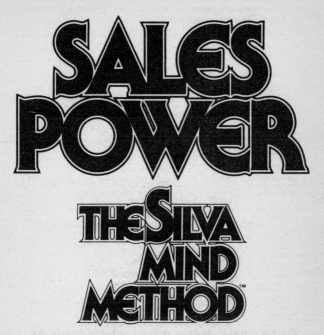

SALES POWER

THE SILVA MIND METHOD™

FOR SALES PROFESSIONALS

JOSÉ SILVA

AND ED BERND, JR.

BERKLEY BOOKS, NEW YORK

SALES POWER

A Berkley Book/published by arrangement with
the authors

PRINTING HISTORY
Perigee Books edition/January 1992
Berkley edition/April 1994

ISBN: 0-425-13474-1

BERKLEY®
Berkley Books are published by The Berkley Publishing Group,
200 Madison Avenue, New York, New York 10016.
BERKLEY and the "B" design
are trademarks belonging to Berkley Publishing Corporation.

PRINTED IN THE UNITED STATES OF AMERICA

10 9 8 7 6 5 4

ACKNOWLEDGMENTS

We would like to give our heartfelt appreciation to Dennis Higgins for his indispensable assistance in writing this book. Dennis is the author of the sales manual used by Silva Method lecturers and organizers, and is a sales consultant to Silva International, Inc.

Dennis, without the support and help you have given so unselfishly for many years, *Sales Power* would never have become a reality.

We also want to thank Hillary Cige for the brilliant, sensitive, and comprehensive job she did in editing the manuscript.

Thanks, Hillary, for making us look so good.

We appreciate all the people who have supported us. We also owe a debt to those who said "No," who opposed us, who told us that we'd never make it, it couldn't be done, we would surely fail; for their opposition helped to make us strong enough to endure and persevere and succeed. We won't name any names . . .

You know who you are.

CONTENTS

	INTRODUCTION	1
1	SALES PSYCHORIENTOLOGY	11
2	THE PRACTICE OF POSITIVE THINKING	29
3	PROFESSIONALISM—LAW OF RATIOS	53
4	IF I'D KNOWN WHERE I WAS GOING I'D HAVE TAKEN A SHORTCUT	79
5	RELAX, IT'S GOOD FOR YOU	99
6	SELF-MANAGEMENT TECHNIQUES	115
7	CREATIVE DREAMING	131
8	CREATIVE VISUALIZATION	147
9	DEVELOPING YOUR PERSONALITY & CHARISMA	181
10	SALES PSYCHOLOGY: WHY PEOPLE BUY	201
11	MAKING THE DEAL	213
12	CREATIVE CLOSING	227
13	HOW CUSTOMER SERVICES INCREASE YOUR INCOME	239
14	OVERCOMING OBJECTIONS AHEAD OF TIME	259

CONTENTS

INTRODUCTION

Throughout history we've admired and honored the super-stars in every field: war heroes, business magnates, out-standing athletes, entertainment celebrities, and of course the super salesmen and -women who seem to be able to find, motivate and persuade people almost by magic.

Have you ever wondered just what makes these super people so much more successful than everyone else?

Sales managers generally agree that in any sales organ-ization, 20 percent of the salespeople make 80 percent of the sales, and 80 percent of the salespeople divide up the remaining 20 percent. Why?

Does that 20 percent work harder? Sure they work hard, yet we all know salespeople who work just as hard, but don't get the same results.

Are they smarter or better educated? Many admit they are not. Some of them have had little formal education.

Is it timing? Again, the answer is no. We see superstars rising and succeeding at all times throughout history. The door of opportunity is always open to those who are ready for it.

If it is not necessarily hard work, or intelligence, or tim-ing, then what *is* the secret to super success? Where is it hidden?

SCIENTISTS SEEK THE SECRET OF SUCCESS

A lot of people have looked. Some have even gotten close to the secret and have observed it without quite being able to put their finger on it. They assign it names like "charisma," and "personal power." And they tell you what they have observed in the hope that you can get some of it for yourself.

A couple of times, people have gotten close to figuring it out. Napoleon Hill, who spent twenty years studying the most successful people in the world, proposed back in 1925 that the key difference was a special mental ability that superstars have. He said they can arouse their minds to go beyond the point at which the average human mind "stops rising or exploring."

"The individual who discovers a way to stimulate his mind artificially, arouse it and cause it to go beyond this average stopping point frequently, is sure to be rewarded with fame and fortune if his efforts are of a constructive nature," Hill wrote.

But Hill never found the answer. In his classic book *Think and Grow Rich* he admits that the secret "has not been directly named" in the book. The closest he could come was to recommend a technique he called the "master mind" concept for creativity, which involved aligning yourself with other people in a synergistic manner.

In the 1960s a group of scientific researchers at the Newark College of Engineering in New Jersey (now New Jersey Institute of Technology), got a little closer to the secret. They spent a decade studying super successful executives to learn what made them different. They used modern electronic equipment and research tools, but they never found the answer. They observed the differences, but they could not put their finger on the cause. The story of their research is detailed in the book *Executive ESP* published by Prentice-Hall in 1974.

Just like Napoleon Hill, the Newark College of Engineering researchers discovered that super successful people possess a special mental ability.

Napoleon Hill even went so far as to say that "the educator who discovers a way to stimulate any mind and cause it to rise above this average stopping point without any bad reactionary effects, will confer a blessing on the human race second to none in the history of the world."

SCIENCE DISCOVERS THE SECRET

Let me tell you a story about the man who answered the question that people have asked since time began:

Why are some few people so much more successful than others?

It was a lay researcher in the border town of Laredo, Texas, who finally found the secret. It took him twenty-two years of some of the toughest, most difficult research ever conducted to uncover it.

He found it in the last place that most people thought to look. He did not find it "out there" somewhere in hard work or goal setting or persistence or some mysterious "extra sense" that some special people have.

The scientist was José Silva.

And José Silva found the secret within the human mind. And more importantly, he found the key to unlock the secret so that all human beings on the planet can use their minds the way the superstars do.

José Silva discovered, and has proven beyond all doubt, that we all have within our own minds, the power to achieve anything we desire. Imagine, you not only have within you the potential to make your dreams come true, you can learn to dream even greater dreams . . . and make them come true also.

So while Napoleon Hill and the researchers at the Newark College of Engineering were observing the one factor that separated the successful from the super successful, José Silva was developing a method to give that same special mental ability to everybody.

A NEW BRANCH OF SCIENCE EMERGES

José Silva began his research into the mind and human potential in 1944. His findings have been available to the public since 1966, and have spawned a whole new field of science, a science called psychorientology (psych'-or-ri-en-tol'-o-gee). Psychorientology is the study of the psyche—the mind—and how to orient it—align it—for success.

In 1966, José Silva authored a forty-hour training program called the Silva Method of Mind Development and Stress Control. As of this writing, the Silva Method is offered in eighty-seven countries and in twenty-one different languages. Millions of people worldwide are successfully using the Silva Method techniques to make their dreams come true.

In 1986, a specialized version of the Silva Method training program was developed just for salespeople. That is what this book is all about—showing you, the salesperson, how to use more of your mind in a special way to get what you really want.

There are no hidden secrets in this book. We spell out for you exactly what the differences are between the average or somewhat successful person and the superstars.

And we give you step-by-step instructions so that you can learn to function the way the superstars do.

In the 1800s the science of psychology grew out of Freud's study of human behavior. Today the study of the human mind—psychorientology—is an equally gigantic leap forward.

Today salespeople need to understand the psychology of selling to rise in their profession.

The superstar salespeople of the future will go beyond that. They will all be sales psychorientologists.

"If you want to be a super salesperson, you've got to know how to understand people and use your greatest and most powerful tool—your mind," says Joe Gandolfo, the number one life insurance salesperson in the world.

Gandolfo was selected as the world's top life insurance salesperson in the best-selling book *Ten Greatest Salespersons* (Harper and Row, 1978).

According to Robert L. Shook, the book's researcher and author, "Gandolfo has been averaging approximately $800 million in sales a year, and in 1975, his biggest year, Gandolfo sold more than a billion dollars' worth. That's like breaking the three-minute mile. Gandolfo's earnings may well be the highest of any salesperson in America."

Gandolfo is one of the natural superstars who recognizes the tremendous contribution José Silva has made.

ADD A NEW DIMENSION TO YOUR SELLING SKILLS

One of the first individuals to apply the new science of psychorientology and add another dimension to his selling skills was Dave Bellizzi of New Jersey. "In 1973, my first full year in the life insurance business, I earned a total of $5,300 in commissions," he recalled. "I was ready to quit. I could have made more working at BurgerKing." Then Dave decided to take action. He attended the Silva Method training program and learned how to use the new science of psychorientology. "Nothing in the program was about selling back then," he said. "All I learned was how to use more of my mind. Once I began to apply what I had learned to selling, selling became easy and fun, and the money began to roll in."

Bellizzi retired in 1983, at the age of thirty, with a net worth of more than $12 million.

Ray Tobias of Chicago was another salesperson who added another dimension to his selling skills. "I did not have much sales ability," Tobias said. "I wasn't well suited for it.'' Yet at the end of his first year as an insurance salesman, the techniques he learned from attending the Silva Method training program helped him to qualify for the award as best new salesman in his company.

Linda Almaraz, a real estate agent with Flair Agency Realtors in Oklahoma, is another salesperson who applies what she has learned from the Silva Method to selling. At the end of her first year as a salesperson, she sold over a million dollars in real estate with the most expensive property being $25,000. That was in 1978. This year (1991) Linda sold one property for $1,800,000. There has not been a home in the State of Oklahoma sold for over a million dollars in the last five years.

Superstars from every field have spoken out about how psychorientology has helped them:

Doc Severinsen, director of the NBC Orchestra on *The Tonight Show*, traveled to Laredo, Texas, to speak at the Silva Method Annual International Convention in 1980.

Bucky Dent, the all-star baseball shortstop of the New York Yankees and most valuable player in the 1978 World Series, said that the Silva Method helped him concentrate better and improve his hitting, and he would recommend it to his younger players.

The Silva Method has also been taught in many colleges and universities throughout the world.

A NEW AND BETTER METHOD

There are countless success stories, many of them told in this book:

- Read how housewife Lyn McKenzie used Silva Method techniques to help her sell corporations and government agencies on funding a service called DateABLE that provides social interaction for handicapped people.
- Share the excitement of an entire group of Mary Kay

Cosmetics sales reps as they soared to unprecedented success—using Silva Method techniques.

- Ken and Elone Hoobler literally had a bank balance of zero, their sales had been so slow. They attended the Silva Method training and their sales soared. Today their business of manufacturing and selling artificial rocks—called Hoobler Stones—is franchised with offices in seventy-five countries!
- Bette Taylor of Austin, Texas, rose from the sales ranks into the executive suite using the Silva Method techniques. Today she has her own consulting business.
- Listen to Garry Kann explain why the Silva Method techniques have been the secret of the success for his new investment banking business.

All of these people, and countless more, learned the Silva Method of Mind Development and now you will too. You have the secret in the palm of your hands—in the pages of this book.

HIGH ACHIEVERS WORK SMARTER

Okay, exactly what does give super successful people their special abilities?

The superstars use both their logical left brain hemisphere and their creative and intuitive right brain hemisphere to think with.

Does this mean that they are twice as successful as the person who uses just one brain hemisphere?

Actually, they are much more than twice as successful.

Imagine that other salespeople thought that they could use only one of their two legs. Just imagine the difficulty they will encounter getting out of a car, or climbing up stairs, or walking into an office. A salesperson who can use both legs possesses far greater skills. With two legs, you could walk right in and make the sale while others are struggling. You could cover far more territory and many more clients. It would seem that you could work miracles compared to the others.

When you learn to use two brains instead of just one, you will start doing things that you would have called miracles back when you were using only your left brain hemisphere to think with.

Some of the techniques that you'll learn in this book will be familiar to you. Remember that you are going to be applying these techniques with two brains instead of just one, the way the most successful people do.

YOU CAN LEARN TO USE MORE OF YOUR BRAIN AND MIND

In the past you have probably made lists of goals and even visualized their completion with some success. A few small obstacles emerged and you took care of them. Next stop: success!

So what happened? You probably encountered the inevitable plateau, the leveling off of your meteoric rise until bigger obstacles emerged and you were not able to surmount them.

Why?

The first great discovery that led to the science of psychorientology answers that question:

The one big difference is that the superstars do their thinking at the alpha brain wave level, so that they can use both brain hemispheres to think with.

What is alpha?

Alpha is a level where the brain waves slow down to about half their normal awake frequency. We put out fourteen to twenty-one brain energy pulsations per second while actively awake. Researchers have called this the beta level. It is the level for action. When you go to sleep you slow down these brain pulsations.

The alpha level has been found to be the ideal level for

thinking. But the average person goes to sleep when their brain enters the alpha level.

Now you can possess this special ability to function consciously at the alpha level and gain access to the untapped powers of your mind. You too can learn how to think with both sides of your brain simultaneously.

You can develop the same *and even greater* creative and intuitive abilities that super-successful people possess.

Now the things that you imagine and visualize will materialize in your life.

Now the techniques recommended by the superstars will work for you because you will be applying them the way the superstars do: at the alpha brain wave level, using both brain hemispheres.

Now you too will be able to get that larger slice of the pie, and all the rewards that go with outstanding achievement. That is what you want, isn't it?

WHAT YOU MUST DO TO SUCCEED

In order to help you use more of your mind to increase your sales and income, you must not only enter the alpha level but also remain there while you apply simple, easy-to-learn techniques.

Just one more thing to succeed: You must make up your mind to invest just fifteen minutes a day in practicing the simple relaxation exercises, and applying the practical mental techniques in this book.

When you do this, you will write your own success story, like our insurance representative Dave Bellizzi. "After earning just $5,300 in 1973, I had concluded that I couldn't make it as a salesman. I was ready to find another job. Then I was introduced to psychorientology and the Silva Method techniques. I learned how to overcome the 'call reluctance' that kept me from seeing more people. I learned how to make better decisions about what to say, when to say it, when to close. Instead of quitting the business, I stuck with it and became very successful.

"In fact," Bellizzi says, "I was making such good decisions about where to invest money that I developed a lucrative financial planning business. At the age of thirty I retired from that business, and now devote my full time to telling other people about the benefits of psychorientology. And even though I am retired from active participation in my business, it still pays me handsomely. My gross income in 1989 was more than $2.7 million."

In this book you will hear exactly how other salespeople, people just like you, actually applied the very same Silva Method techniques that you will learn, and dramatically increased their sales and income. They explain what they did, and how they did it. Then José Silva shows you exactly how you can do it too.

This is actually two books in one. Dennis Higgins, sales trainer and consultant for Silva International, Inc., provides many proven sales strategies, while José Silva shows you how to use your special mental abilities to make these strategies work even better. Ed Bernd Jr., Silva Method marketing coordinator and editor of the company's newsletter, gathered the success stories, coordinated the project, and did most of the actual writing. Special sections of the book have been written exclusively by José Silva, in which he will personally teach you his method of mind development.

You are beginning this book at the exact moment in time for unlimited achievement. Timing is always the easiest ingredient in your personal recipe for success.

The greatest discovery you will ever make . . . is the potential of your own mind.

1

SALES PSYCHORIENTOLOGY

Pat walked easily across the lobby, her steps firm, exchanging smiles as she saw people she had met on previous visits.

This could be her biggest sale of the year, a sale sought by at least two dozen other salespeople.

They had a product just as good as Pat's, and some of them were much older and had been in the business a lot longer. As she approached Mr. Simmons' secretary, Pat did not have to make an effort to appear relaxed; she really was relaxed.

Pat possessed a secret weapon that enabled her to know exactly how to approach Mr. Simmons and exactly what to say to him: Sales Psychorientology.

During the last few nights, Pat had relaxed at home and thought about all the different approaches she could use, thought about what Mr. Simmons' reaction to each of them would be. She thought about all of the information she had gathered about Mr. Simmons and his company, and what he wanted from her product. She thought about what Mr. Simmons had told her that he wanted; she also thought about the things he had not told her, the things she had figured out with the use of Sales Psychorientology.

Several times over the last few days Pat had awakened during the night and used the Sales Psychorientology techniques to help her gain new insight and understanding into

Mr. Simmons' situation, and his reasons for wanting things done his way.

It was not nervousness that had awakened Pat to think about this sale. It was part of her regular routine, her Sales Psychorientology routine, to spend some quiet time figuring out her approach. After learning all that she could through research and interviews, Pat knew that she could trust her instincts.

"It's almost like cheating," she said. "I know what the client wants, what his objections will be and how I can answer them and satisfy him. I know what he can really afford, no matter what he might have told me."

But it had not always been that way for Pat.

When she first entered the sales profession, it would be an effort for Pat to keep from hyperventilating before she entered the building. The massive walls were hostile. Doors loomed like threatening barricades. Deep, plush carpet gripped her feet like quicksand. The secretary blocking the way resurrected the specter of cruel schoolmates who loved to embarrass Pat in front of the other children.

In the beginning of her sales career, Pat did not view the telephone as a friend, as a valuable tool that would put money in her pocket. Instead, the telephone's alarm would set her heart racing, her lungs gasping for air, would make her muscles tense up as she braced herself for the impending confrontation and expected rejection.

What made the difference?

Pat learned techniques to help her control her anxiety and fears. She learned how to use mental rehearsal, not only to help her project confidence, but to actually *be* confident. She learned powerful stress management techniques to help her relax in any circumstances.

Pat learned how to channel her personal energies so that she could perform to her maximum potential any time, under any conditions.

She learned how to actually develop and maintain a positive mental attitude no matter what might be happening around her.

She learned to overcome limiting belief systems that had

always hampered her and held her back.

She learned to use more of her mind in a special way and to trust her intuition.

Pat was introduced to the new science of psychorientology, and how to apply Sales Psychorientology to her profession.

THE GENIUS WITHIN

It is relatively easy for you to take control of your intellect and use it. But what about your feelings, your emotions? Is there someone else inside each of us, a part of us we hardly know, that is in charge of feelings, instincts, emotions, intuition?

Are we really two people?

Yes, we are. In fact, we are really three people. Sigmund Freud identified them as Ego, Superego, and Id. Eric Berne identified them as Parent, Adult, and Child. Both of those models are somewhat limited when compared to the model that Dr. J. Wilfred Hahn came up with.

Dr. Hahn is a biochemist by training, and a parapsychology researcher by inclination. He has served as a valuable Silva Method scientific consultant for more than three decades, and is one of the leading researchers in the new science of psychorientology.

Dr. Hahn realized a long time ago that a part of him believes in education and science and the things of the physical world that he can see, hear, smell, taste, and touch; while another part of him believes in fun without understanding why it is fun, that believes in love without being able to prove that love in a laboratory, that believes in intuition even when it cannot be verified by standard scientific criteria.

WILLIE, WILFRED AND WILL

To help him understand himself better, Dr. Hahn decided to refer to the serious, intellectual side of himself as Wilfred, and the playful, creative and intuitive side of himself as Willie. And he realized that there is a director at some level higher than either Wilfred or Willie. He calls the director Will.

There is some irony here. Our conventional educational systems and processes concentrate on teaching Wilfred, on making changes (and hopefully improvements) to the intellectual side of us. That's what happens in school, and in the pages of every sales training book you have read . . . before this one.

What about Willie? How do you learn to manage your feelings, your instincts, your creativity, your emotions, your intuition? How do you learn to orient and direct your mind toward solving problems in your life and achieving outstanding success?

HOW DAVE BELLIZZI MADE HIS DREAMS COME TRUE

"After graduating college in 1972," Dave Bellizzi related, "I began my sales career as a representative for a major life insurance company. The first six months in the business I sold $1 million worth of insurance . . . to my friends and acquaintances. I made almost $70,000 in those first six months and thought this was the greatest job in the world.

"The next year, I made a total of $5,300 for the entire year," he continued. "I ran out of friends and acquaintances. I realized that I knew nothing about selling. So I went out and bought every sales book I could get my hands on. I went to sales seminars and bought all of the tapes and everything else. I even found out who the world's number one life insurance salesman was and learned everything he did. I learned his best prospecting techniques, his best approaches, his best closing techniques, how he effectively handled objections . . . everything.

"Nothing helped. People turned me down for appointments, and the people I did get to see wouldn't buy when I tried to close. I couldn't figure it out. I was ready to quit.

"Then I found out that my real problem was something called fear of rejection and call reluctance. I lacked self-confidence. I had a poor self-image. So I went out and bought all the top motivational books and tapes on the market. They got me all fired up to make the calls, but after the first couple of rejections, I was back to square one again.

OVERCOMING LIMITING BELIEF SYSTEMS

"Then I went to a psychologist to see if he could help me overcome my problem. No results. I knew the problem was all in my mind, but I didn't know what to do about it. The psychologist wasn't much help.

"So one Wednesday night in 1974, after much anguish and turmoil, I decided to type up my resignation and hand it in to my manager the next day. I even failed at that . . . when I went to the office on Thursday, my sales manager had called in sick. He would be back on Friday, so I decided to wait one more day. And that was the best thing that could have happened to me.

"I spent all day Thursday looking through the newspaper want ads. While going through one particular paper I came across an ad about a program called the Silva Method that claimed to show people how to use more of their minds. They were conducting a free introductory seminar that same night. I decided to check it out.

"It wasn't even a sales training program, but after hearing their spiel, I decided to take the program and see if it could help me increase my sales.

"Within ninety days after completing the program my sales increased 200 percent. I was able to combine the skills and techniques that I had learned in the Silva Method with the skills and techniques I had learned from the world's number one life insurance agent to dramatically increase my sales production. Selling was easy and fun again.

"In 1978, after having a lot of success selling life insurance, I decided to start my own financial planning practice. Using the Silva Method skills and techniques I was able to build a multimillion-dollar financial planning firm.''

A TECHNIQUE TO HELP YOU ACHIEVE MORE PERSONAL GROWTH

Would you like to have a special technique to help you get 100 percent more benefit from this book—and from any self-improvement program you take? This technique comes from Alejandro Gonzalez Jr. who is Senior Vice President, Administrator, and General Manager of Silva International, Inc.

Gonzalez retired from the Air Force as a Senior Master Sergeant with twenty-two years' experience of dealing with people and motivating them.

''As a businessman,'' he explains, ''if I send an employee to a seminar to learn some new techniques to use in business, then after the employee completes the seminar I take certain specific steps to insure that we get our money's worth from our investment.

''Here's what I do: I put that employee in charge of a project where he has to use the new skills. I might put him in charge of ten other employees and let him know I expect him to produce.

''In other words, I let the employee know that I expect more from him than I received in the past, and I set up a situation to achieve that result.''

Make up your mind to take that same approach. Set new goals for yourself. Line up projects and make a commitment to succeed at those projects. Give yourself a project that will test your abilities a bit, one that will require you to use the new mental techniques that you will learn in this book in order to succeed.

MAKE YOUR DREAMS COME TRUE
WITH PSYCHORIENTOLOGY

Using psychorientology to increase sales has helped many people build prosperous businesses of their own.

One of the first examples was Ken and Elone Hoobler. "In 1970, when we lived in Irving, Texas, we studied José Silva's Silva Method," Ken recalled. "Our whole lives changed." They now own their own successful business marketing artificial decorative stones called Hoobler Stones, used by builders in more than sixty nations.

"When we finished the Silva Method training," they said, "José Silva asked many of the graduates what they intended to do with the techniques, now that they learned how to use more of their minds."

Ken told José, "I intend to see all the world and almost every country in the world."

"José Silva gave us the key," they explained. He told them, "You work so hard to do all the things that you do. Why don't you use more from your neck up instead of down?"

They took his suggestion seriously. The results? "We have completely circled the world three different times in three different routes," the Hooblers said. "Our trips always pay for themselves and more, because that is the way we program it."

The Hooblers like to help people, and to spread the word about how everyone can learn to use more mind for a better and better life.

They are good salespeople. You have heard about the salesman who could sell refrigerators to Eskimos? The Hooblers have sold this American form of "Dynamic Meditation" to residents of India!

John and Rita Donohue also used psychorientology to build their own business, called Magic Wind. They make and sell wind chimes and other items.

Their dream grew from a business grossing a little over $26,000 in 1976 to more than $300,000 in 1981 and was closing in on $1 million a year later.

"Perhaps the most significant factor of 1976," they said, "was an encounter with a powerful problem-solving technique called the Silva Method of Mind Development. The use of this meditation/visualization skill through the years has been a priceless asset for growth and a vital factor in the success of the business."

"There is no way to estimate the value of the Silva Method principles in the conduct of a business," they added. "We have found the Silva Method of Mind Development to be the most grounded, practical, accessible, and easy method of all the self-improvement programs we have attended."

Californian Kitt Curtis is another Silva Method graduate who started her own business. Along with her daughter Geri, and Betty Ash, she owns a coffee-roasting plant. Published reports list them as the only women in the world with their own coffee roasting plant. "Thank you, José Silva, that class helped me *so* much," Curtis wrote in an unsolicited testimonial.

HOW LIMITATIONS ARE BORN

How is Willie trained? One way to train Willie is the same way you train an elephant.

Have you ever been to a circus and seen the elephants tied up outside the circus tents? A small rope ties the elephant's leg to a small stake that has been tapped into the ground.

How does this stake hold the elephant? After all, when a wild elephant is hungry, it doesn't bother reaching up to the top of the tree for its food; it just pushes the tree over so the tasty leaves are at a more convenient level.

How can an animal so big and powerful be controlled

by a rope tied to a little stake?

Training. When the elephant was very small, the trainer used a big chain attached securely to a big post hammered deep into the ground to limit the elephant's movement. The elephant could only go so far, and it was not big enough or strong enough to break the chain or pull up the stake.

The elephant quickly learned its limits: It could only go to the end of the chain that was locked to its leg.

With our intellect, we know that a fully grown elephant could easily break the rope or uproot the stake that holds it, but since no one has communicated that to the elephant, it remains within its limits.

Can this happen to a human being?

Think about this:

When you were a young child, in school, and your parents and teachers loved you and wanted to motivate you to do your best, did they ever equate your grades in school to your ability to succeed in life as a grown-up: "You must study hard and make good grades if you want to be a success in life."

If you are like most people, your grades were probably average. After all, they set up the system so that only a few people made good grades, and only a few made really bad grades. Most people were average. They learned their limits early. They learned their limits at an age when very strong impressions are being made on the brain, impressions that will lie buried, shaping our lives, after the brain matures and is functioning more intellectually.

Our grown-up intellect "knows" that we need not be limited by the grades we made in school many years ago. We have many examples: José Silva never got a grade, because he never went to school a day in his life . . . as a student. Einstein failed math. Helen Keller was thought to be unteachable.

So we "know" that we do not have to be limited. But nobody is getting the message through to Willie. It was the young, emotional, feeling, helpless Willie who got the message. And Willie is still working hard to keep us within those limits.

Willie can bring your progress to a dead stop, just as the rope stops the circus elephant.

On the other hand, Willie can work for you, twenty-four hours a day every day of your life, to help you make all of your dreams come true. In fact, you can do more than make your dreams come true . . . you can learn to dream greater dreams.

RE-PROGRAMMING YOUR BIOCOMPUTER FOR GREATER SUCCESS

To help you understand how you, as a human being, function, let's just consider the brain for a moment. Your brain functions much like a computer. It operates on a very small amount of electrical energy that pulses, or beats, several times each second. Like a computer, your brain can store information and retrieve that information later. That's called memory. And when programmed properly, your brain can use information to solve problems.

Your brain has many highly specialized areas. The cortex—the wrinkled-up gray matter that forms the outer portion of your brain—is divided into two halves: the left brain hemisphere, and the right brain hemisphere.

The left brain hemisphere is associated with logical, rational thought; with the objective—physical—senses. The left brain hemisphere must understand everything, must have a reason for everything. This is the part used mostly by Wilfred.

The right brain hemisphere is associated with imagination, creativity, and intuition. This side of your brain sees patterns and form. It appreciates art and music. You could say that your left brain hemisphere sees the trees, while the right brain hemisphere sees the forest. Your right brain hemisphere is associated with your subjective—mental—senses. It is used mostly by Willie.

To achieve your full potential, you need to use both brain hemispheres to think with, to use both Wilfred and Willie, working together as partners. You need Wilfred's logic and ability to reason, and you also need Willie's creativity and intuition.

But most people use only the logical left brain hemisphere. They develop their physical senses to a high degree, but virtually ignore their mental senses.

MULTIPLY YOUR TALENT— AUTOMATICALLY

When you learn to use both your left and your right brain hemispheres as they are meant to be used, instead of just using only your left brain hemisphere, you will be infinitely more successful.

Let's look at it this way:

Suppose you were one of several salespeople going to make a presentation to a prospect, and the other salespeople all thought that they could use only one leg. While all the others were hopping around, trying to get along on just half of their abilities, you would look like a person who was in control and who could get things done.

To them, it would seem like you could work miracles. Even if you cannot run fast, you can still outrun a person who uses only one leg. Even if they use crutches, you could still outperform them so much it would seem to them like you were working miracles.

But, if they only knew they could use their other leg, they too could do the things you do. They could make more sales, help more people, and everyone would be better off.

That is what it is like when you learn to use both brain hemispheres to think with. You will be doing things you used to think were miracles, things you thought you could never do, things you thought were done only by special people with something "extra."

You have both a left and a right brain hemisphere, just like everyone else. You have a mind just like everyone else. You can learn to use more of your mind, the way the superstars do. Just imagine how this can help you and your loved ones.

The greatest discovery you will ever make, is the potential of your own mind.

EVERYONE CAN SUCCEED

If you feel a little bit skeptical about learning to use intuition to help you, that is all right. It is Wilfred who is the skeptic. That is Wilfred's job, to protect us by screening everything for us and helping us to avoid things that might hurt us or waste our time or money.

In fact, there is no logical way to convince Wilfred about intuition and creativity and other nonphysical things. Wilfred's domain is the physical world.

But the Silva Method techniques will work for you, because you will begin to learn shortly how to bypass Wilfred and gain direct access to Willie. Then you will give new instructions to Willie, and this will enable you to function the way the superstars do.

At that time, Wilfred will accept the reality of your experience, although there might still be a tendency to want to find an explanation.

RESEARCH SHOWS THAT EVEN SKEPTICS SUCCEED

A research study conducted by Rafael Liberman at the Sociology Department of Bar-Illan University in Israel showed that both skeptics and believers attained equally good results in attaining the goals they were seeking from the Silva Method techniques.

Both believers and skeptics attained a similar number of objectives, Liberman reported. But there was one difference: Those with a high expectation reported greater success within the individual fields, than the group with low expectations.

According to Liberman, "The results show that 'skeptics' who take the Silva course attain the same achievements as those whose expectations were high."

To gain the greatest benefit from the techniques in this book, simply recognize that Wilfred will be skeptical from time to time, and that's all right. All you need to do to be successful is to make up your mind to follow the instructions, and you will succeed. We guarantee it.

CONTROLLING THE SUBCONSCIOUS, CONSCIOUSLY

In order to re-educate Willie, we must first get Wilfred to be quiet. Wilfred is like a manager who demands to be heard. When Wilfred barks out orders, Willie has to listen and usually must obey.

But Wilfred has some rather severe limitations. Wilfred has some very strong needs: the need to prove everything logically, the need to do things in sequence, the need to explain things rationally, the need to be in control.

Willie, on the other hand, is creative, intuitive, trusting. And Wilfred is suspicious of much of what Willie does. Wilfred does not understand creativity, because so often it comes in illogical ways. Wilfred does not trust intuition because it cannot be explained by conventional scientific criteria. Wilfred has little respect for anyone who does not fight to be in control.

Yet Willie is the one who knows how to carry out the instructions that Wilfred gives. When Wilfred wants to store some information away in memory, for instance, Willie takes care of the task, and Wilfred does not have a clue as to where Willie stores things. When Wilfred needs a solution, Willie can get it without Wilfred having any idea of how it was done. Of course, Wilfred has such a strong need to explain everything that Wilfred will come up with an explanation, even if it is not true.

How do you mediate between these two aspects of yourself?

Through an act of Will.

As you practice the techniques in this book, you will learn how to contact your higher self, the part of you that is in contact with higher intelligence and can guide you to do what is best, not only for yourself, but for all concerned.

You can achieve more through cooperation than by confrontation.

There is enough of everything for everyone. When you see things from a higher perspective, you will know exactly how to use both Wilfred and Willie appropriately to get whatever you need and do what is best for all concerned.

José Silva believes that we were assigned to this planet in order to help correct problems. The more problems we correct, the more rewards we will receive.

When you do what you are supposed to be doing, he says, you will be rewarded. That is how high intelligence lets us know we are doing what we should be doing.

All this is easier to do than explain, so let's get right on to your first mental training exercise, also known as a conditioning cycle. For that, we will turn the floor over to José Silva:

TRAINING YOUR MIND

So you have agreed to set aside fifteen minutes every day to develop and acquire the extra ability to function consciously at alpha.

Now let's start. In the forty-hour Silva Method training program, attendees learn how to function consciously at alpha in just a few hours, because they have the help of a trained lecturer who guides them step-by-step and answers all of their questions. Since you are going to be learning by reading this book, it will take longer. It will take you approximately forty days.

I am going to let you begin the Silva Method for increased sales by using positive mental instructions while relaxed.

I will give you a simple way to relax, and you will do better and better at this as you practice.

I will also give you a simple statement to affirm to yourself.

This is how you educate Willie. You relax, get Wilfred to be quiet, lower your brain frequency to the alpha range where Willie resides, and communicate directly with Willie.

What do we mean by alpha brain wave frequencies?

Your brain operates on a small amount of electricity that pulses several times a second. During the day, when you are functioning at the outer conscious level of mind, your brain pulses about twenty times a second (cycles per second, or cps). When you go to sleep at night, your brain pulsing slows down to one time per second, or less.

Alpha is in the center of this normal daily frequency range, about ten cycles per second. This is associated with light sleep, dreams, and relaxed daydreaming.

The mental exercise I am going to show you now will help you learn to lower your brain frequency while maintaining conscious awareness. In other words, you are going to learn how to work with both Wilfred and Willie at the same time, with conscious awareness in both dimensions. When Wilfred and Willie begin working together, instead of at odds with each other as they often do, you will begin to get results in your life that seem like miracles.

I will show you a simple mental exercise now to get you started.

Even though you are going to be a beginner at this, expect a miracle.

Your desire, belief, and expectations are the "green light" to Willie to go ahead and start changing your life for the better.

On the other hand, if you are saying to yourself, "Well, I'll do the exercise, but I don't really think it is going to do any good," that's Wilfred wanting to remain in control and block access to Willie. If that happens, just acknowledge that this is okay, Wilfred is doing his job. Then go ahead and relax, do the exercise confidently, and it will work.

The choice is yours, through an act of Will.

The moment of decision has come.

Do you want to be more in charge of your life?

If your answer is yes, your dividends can be not only in increased sales, but in every other facet of your life as well: better health, better relationships, and all the other things that help you enjoy life more.

Since you cannot read this book and relax simultaneously, it is necessary that you read the instructions first, so that you can put the book down, close your eyes, and follow them. Here they are:

YOUR FIRST ALPHA EXPERIENCE

1. Sit comfortably in a chair and close your eyes. Any position that is comfortable is a good position.
2. Take a deep breath and as you exhale relax your body.
3. Count backwards slowly from 50 to 1.
4. Daydream about some peaceful place you know.
5. Say to yourself mentally, "Every day in every way I am getting better, better, and better."
6. Remind yourself that when you open your eyes at the count of 5, you will feel wide awake, better than before. When you reach the count of 3, repeat this, and when you open your eyes affirm it again ("I am wide awake, feeling better than before").

You already know steps 1 and 2. You do it daily when you get home from work. Add a countdown, a peaceful scene, and an affirmation to help you become better and better and you are ready for a final count-out.

Read the instructions once more. Then put the book down and do it . . .

THE MAGIC OF THINKING AT ALPHA

Thanks to Mr. Silva, you have just experienced "programming."

Your ability to program gets better with practice. With practice, you relax more quickly and you reach deeper levels of mind; you visualize more realistically; your levels of expectation and belief heighten, yielding bigger and better results.

Programming in this manner at the alpha dimension produces far better results than programming at beta.

You can repeat affirmations a thousand times at the outer level, where Wilfred filters everything through his analytical processes, and not have as much effect on Willie as you can with just one repetition at the alpha level, where Willie resides.

That is the secret of why some people are able to visualize their goals and reach them, while most people get very little result.

Silva Method research has found that only about one person in ten naturally thinks at the alpha brain wave level, and acts at the beta level. Remember, the only way to get superior results is to learn how to do your thinking at the alpha level, the way the ten-percenters do.

HOW YOU CAN BECOME A SUPERSTAR

When you practiced the simple relaxation exercise a few minutes ago, you took the very first step in causing your mind "to go beyond this average stopping point."

And as you continue with the exercises in this book, you are "sure to be rewarded with fame and fortune" if your efforts are of a constructive nature.

Napoleon Hill knew it in 1925, but he didn't know how to teach it. And in *Think and Grow Rich* two decades later he still couldn't explain how to do it.

The Silva Method is the program that can "stimulate any mind and cause it to rise above this average point without any bad reactionary effects." It is the first program in history to achieve this.

And now you can achieve this, just like the superstars. It is yours if you will invest just fifteen minutes a day in practice, if you will ask Wilfred to stand by while you communicate directly with Willie.

Now that you have completed that first brief mental exercise, you are ready to go to the next chapter and learn to "concentrate" even better.

YOUR STEP-BY-STEP ROADMAP TO SUCCESS

We will be with you and guide you every step of the way until, as you approach the end of the book, you will be able to take control of your life and live the way you desire. You will be able to help yourself, and know how you can use your mind's energy to program other people at a distance to help them, also.

And isn't that what selling is all about: Helping people get what they want through the use of your product or service.

It is as easy as A, B, C.

And it all starts with alpha.

2

THE PRACTICE OF POSITIVE THINKING

A company once sent a shoe salesman to a township in Africa where they had never sold any shoes. He was one of their senior, most experienced salesmen, and they expected big things of him.

Shortly after his arrival in Africa, he wrote the home office saying, "You might as well bring me back. Nobody here wears shoes."

They brought him back.

Then they sent another shoe salesman. This time, they sent one of their newest salesmen. He did not have much experience, but he had a lot of enthusiasm. They figured he might be able to sell a few pairs of shoes.

Almost as soon as he arrived, he wired the home office an urgent message: "Send me all the shoes you've got. Nobody here is wearing shoes!"

HERE'S HOW POSITIVE THINKING HELPS YOU GET WHAT YOU WANT

A positive statement is a statement about what you want, rather than what you don't want.

Consider this: A child is running toward the door, and

you know that his exit is likely to be a noisy one. So you give a command: "Don't slam the door!"

Now in those words—"Don't slam the door"—what scenario do you imagine? What picture is likely to be constructed out of those words?

A slamming door, of course.

That's because a negative statement was used. Negative does not mean it was bad; it means that the statement gave the opposite image of what we desired.

How would you phrase the request as a positive statement? Think about it for a moment. There are several ways.

You could say, "Please close the door gently," or "Please go out quietly." Those are positive statements, because the words create mental pictures of what we want.

The word "Don't" signals that a negative statement is coming. We have to stop and think about it, reverse it, figure out what we *do* desire in order to make a positive mental picture for the brain to act on.

Imagine how important it is in a selling situation to use positive statements. It is very valuable to keep using words that create the mental pictures you want your prospect to have.

POSITIVE THINKING TURNS REJECTION INTO SUCCESS

Does this work in the real world?

It worked quite well for San Antonio, Texas, radio announcer Steve Sellers. "We project a positive image to our listeners by eliminating the negatives," Sellers explained. "Other stations' weathercasters announce a partly cloudy day—on our station that same day is partly sunny." Within thirty days of starting this approach the station, which for years had been the overlooked stepchild in the broadcasting chain, turned into a viable force in the San Antonio radio market.

It worked well for Ray Tobias of Chicago.

"I started work as an insurance rep for Franklin Life Insurance Company right after I took the Silva Method training," Tobias said. "I was green, didn't know where I was going, I was even skeptical about selling anything, because I had not been a sales oriented person."

First he used the speed learning techniques he learned in the Silva Method Basic Lecture Series to help him complete the life insurance company's sales training program.

Then he used the Silva Method techniques to prepare himself for sales calls, to be ready to satisfy the client's need. "I improved myself to a point where I received the award as the highest first year sales rep for the agency," he said.

"In fact I did so well that the manager wanted me to teach the Silva techniques to all the other reps. We got a training program where I did a talk to the other reps. After that, whenever I called the manager, if I said anything negative, he would immediately say, 'Cancel-cancel,' and 'Better and better.' All the reps were doing that. Those who did it improved. Those who didn't, didn't see much of a change.

"I did not program to get the award," he added. "I didn't even know there was an award. Each time I'd go out, I'd program to do what needed to be done to be successful; to satisfy the needs of the prospect, to do what was in his best interest, and that we would be of some good for him.

"I would program that, 'I will think the thoughts, speak the words, and perform the actions that will be well received by this prospect, and also work for their best interest.'

"When things weren't going so well, like a couple of turn downs, or a couple of 'I'll get back to you' answers, or 'See me later,' and I'd get depressed and think, 'Oh, he'll never get back,' I'd do a mental housecleaning. I'd use 'Cancel-cancel' a lot.

"Then I'd flush out all the negative things after the day was over, things which might in any way affect my success. I'd imagine doing it the way that would be successful, that would also be well received, and would be important to that prospect.

"Each prospect is different. You can't take it out of a manual. Where it says to follow this script, you can't do that. Each person is unique. So I wanted to reach those particular needs.

"Whenever one of the salesmen would say something negative, like, 'Oh, I probably won't get this one,' or 'I probably won't make this sale,' or 'I'm doing real lousy,' I'd say, 'Cancel-cancel.'

"This was the best agency of all the agencies. The morale was great. The guys were always high, were always up. We had the most sales and best morale of the ten agencies in our region.

"At the awards banquet," Tobias recalled, "I didn't know I was going to get this award, for most productive. Not bad for somebody without much aptitude for sales."

WRONG PICTURE LOSES THE SALE

"I once heard an insurance salesman use what he thought was a very positive approach to make a tough sale," Dave Bellizzi recalled. "After he had run out of other ideas, he said to the man, 'You don't want your wife to be a poor widow, do you?' But look at what kind of picture that created in the prospect's mind. It was a terrible picture, the last thing the prospect wanted to see. He threw the salesman out.

"What he could have said to create a positive picture," Bellizzi continued, "is something like this: 'If you die your wife will have enough money to maintain your present lifestyle.' Or he could have said, 'She will have enough money to put your children through college. That *is* what you want, isn't it?'"

Always check your statements and presentations and determine whether they are creating mental pictures of things that make people feel good.

A SIMPLE CHANGE IN ATTITUDE MADE THEM WINNERS

Hector Chacon, a high school basketball coach, found himself slipping into the habit of thinking more about mistakes than he was about successes. He changed his ways and used the psychorientology approach to positive thinking to motivate an entire team.

"We probably all start off thinking about winning," Chacon said. "We dream the great dreams. And in the beginning, we probably don't even recognize the mistakes we make.

"But as we gain more and more skill and experience," he continued, "we begin to concentrate more and more on playing the perfect game, eliminating every mistake. And that can be dangerous.

"When we stop focusing on the end result that we desire, and start thinking instead about mistakes, we are likely to make more mistakes."

That's exactly what happened to Coach Chacon. His team would build up a lead in the first half. At halftime he would focus on the errors in an attempt to correct them. He'd confront the players with their mistakes and challenge them to correct them. All the mental pictures were negative—pictures of the problem. They would blow the lead and lose the game.

After the first five conference games, they were 1–4.

Then the coach changed his way of talking to his players. "I called on a friend of mine who had taken the Silva Method, and asked if he had any ideas that could help me," Coach Chacon said. "He spent twenty minutes on the phone with me, explaining the principles of positive thinking." As a result, Chacon made up his mind to avoid confrontation and instead compliment his players and seek their cooperation.

"In that night's game, I still pointed out the mistakes,"

he said, "but after that, I made sure that I told the players exactly what I wanted them to do. And I took it one step further. I reminded each player of a successful play he had made, and told them to do it like that again."

The results? The first time out with this psychorientology technique, they beat a team that had beaten them a few weeks earlier. They beat them by a score of 80 to 47! In their final nine conference games, after that one simple change in Coach Chacon's approach, they had an 8–1 record.

OPERATING YOUR BIO-COMPUTER BRAIN

We mentioned earlier that your brain stores information, much as a computer does. And you can retrieve (recall) that information, and can use it to make decisions and solve problems.

Of course, the quality of the decisions, and the quality of the solutions, is only as good as the quality of the data that you use when making the decisions and selecting the solutions.

In the computer business they use the term GIGO to represent this: Garbage In, Garbage Out.

The information that you put into the computer is the information that you use to make decisions and select solutions.

If you put bad data in, you get bad output.

This applies to your brain just as it does to any other computer.

If you want to be a superstar sales professional, make up your mind now to put data and information into your computer that will provide you with the answers and solutions that will help you reach that goal. It will pay you dividends to read inspiring books that help you perform better, instead of reading about "born losers" and other failures. It will be much smarter to associate with Winners rather than sit around with the losers and complain about how unfair life is.

HOW TO PLANT SEEDS OF SUCCESS IN YOUR MIND

Let's think for a moment about where the data comes from that you put into your bio-computer's memory banks. If you are going to make withdrawals from your memory bank, you want to be sure to make good deposits to that memory bank.

Data can come from things you read, things you hear, movies and television programs you watch, experiences that you have. Where else?

All of the items we have listed so far have one thing in common: They are all physical things, things that exist in the physical dimension. There is another whole category of data that goes into your memory bank and is used for decision making, goal setting, and problem solving.

What about the things you think?

If you think that you might fail to make a sale, does that thought go into your memory bank? Can you recall later that you had that thought? Of course you can.

And what about if you think of success: Does that thought go into your memory bank? Can you recall it later? Of course.

TRADE IN YOUR OLD WEAKNESSES FOR POWERFUL NEW STRENGTHS

If you recall a time when you did not make a sale, and you experience fear when you think about the next sales presentation you are going to make, then you are putting data into your bio-computer that could cause you to make decisions and to behave in a way that will cause you to fail to make the sale. Fear is a very powerful energizer, and it is contagious.

If you make up your mind to put as much energy into

thinking of a time when you made a big exciting sale, and you get excited all over again, then you are putting data into your bio-computer that can result in decisions that will help you make the sale. You will select the right words, use the correct gestures and facial expressions and voice inflections. Your body and your whole aura will be programmed automatically to help you make the sale.

POSITIVE THINKING SAVED LOST SALES AND A BUSINESS

"Last summer, we were just about broke," Chuck Warnock said. "Our photography business wasn't going well, we weren't making enough profit, and I thought we might go under. Debbie remembered hearing Carolyn Deal at a Silva Method introductory lecture and called her. Debbie enrolled in the next Silva course, and the rest is history.

"A year later, our company was named 'Franchise of the Year' by the home office," Chuck said. "We were competing with 104 other franchise owners, and weren't even expecting to be nominated, much less selected."

"Chuck wasn't real gung-ho about the Silva Method at first," his wife Debbie said. "So I took it, and he watched to see what would happen. When he saw that what I was doing seemed to be making a difference in what he was doing, then he took the course too."

Positive thinking has been very important, as Debbie explained in the following example.

"In our business, we go to churches and take pictures of all the families. Then we make a pictorial directory for the church, for free.

"We are allowed to go back and sell copies of the portraits to the members. If they don't buy the portraits, then we do, so it is very important to sell the portraits."

On one occasion, they had a problem. "The photographer wasn't aware of it at the time, but one of the strobe lights was not flashing. As a result, the lighting was off terribly in all the photos. They looked like mug shots, that should have been hung in the post office.

"They were the worst looking pictures I have ever seen. The lighting caused people to have a really harsh look. They had shadows on their faces that showed the bags under their eyes and everything.

"The hardest thing to sell is a picture like that. Women, especially, will say, 'Well, I don't like these because I am getting older, and it looks like I am getting older.'

"So we knew we had a problem before we went to sell these. We knew that we had a possibility of losing a whole lot of money in that particular church."

They programmed themselves; they imagined everyone being happy with the pictures, looking at the good things about them: the pictures were of a very special occasion involving church and family, it was a very special moment in their lives, and they wanted the pictures to remember it by.

Armed with that positive programming, the photographer went back with the pictures. "He had the highest sales average he'd ever had in any church," Debbie said. "Not one person declined to buy. Nobody said anything about the pictures looking bad.

"We did not let an error in the photo session ruin the joy that those families should have with the pictures of that special occasion.

"That encouraged us to keep on, to keep being positive, not trying to judge what people would like or not like, what they could afford or not afford. We just keep a positive attitude, and program that people will want the pictures. It is working pretty good for us."

Warnock was a pastor for thirty years. At this writing, the former Silva Method skeptic and his wife are considering becoming Silva Method instructors.

"I think that Silva is a very spiritual thing," Debbie explained. "What I like about it is, I think that God made us this way. All this stuff is not something that José Silva invented. He just figured out that this is the way human beings are made.

"As I see it," she said, "we are just tapping into things that God already put there. We just didn't know how to use it yet, didn't have an instruction manual on it."

RESEARCH PROVES HOW YOUR EXPECTANCY GETS RESULTS— GOOD OR BAD

If you want scientific proof of how your expectancy can affect someone else, check out the research that was conducted by Dr. Robert Rosenthal of the University of North Dakota several years ago.

In this project, which is well known among educators, Dr. Rosenthal set out to determine the effect of a person's expectations on research subjects. The research subjects he chose were laboratory rats.

In this carefully controlled experiment, twelve senior division students in experimental psychology were each assigned a group of five albino rats to run through a maze ten times a day for five days. Although the rats were selected at random, each student was informed that the rats were either "maze-bright" or "maze-dull."

The results, reported by Ernest O. Melby in the book *The Teacher and Learning*, indicated that "on three of the five days and for the experiment as a whole, experimenters believing their subjects to be bright obtained performance from them significantly superior to that obtained by experimenters believing their subjects to be dull. The subjects believed to be bright appeared to be learning the problem while those believed to be dull did not."

If a person's expectations can have that much effect on a rat, imagine the effect it can have on another person.

Make up your mind to expect the best, and you will usually get it.

PROOF POSITIVE IS IN YOUR HANDS

There is a simple experiment you can conduct to dramatically demonstrate the power that words have over your physical body.

Roy Proctor was an insurance salesman for many years in San Antonio, Texas. After he took the Silva Method training in 1970, Roy and his wife Maree moved to New Orleans to open a Silva Method center there. Positive thoughts can make you stronger and negative thoughts can make you weaker. Roy and Maree Proctor can prove that to you.

To demonstrate the effect that words have on a person, they will first test the strength of a person's skeletal muscles, then have them use certain words and note the changes.

"A seaman came to our Silva Method lectures one time," Maree recalled. "He used the word 'damn' extensively. I called him on it, and he looked defensive, like, 'Lady, if you can't take it . . . ' We had him get up and hold his arm out, while I measured how much force it took to push the arm down. Then I had him repeat the word while I pushed down on his arm again. There was a dramatic difference in strength: He was weaker every time we tested him."

You can conduct the same experiment using the words "can" and "can't."

To test yourself, you will need an assistant to measure your strength. There are two easy ways to do this: Either hold your arm straight out to your side, with your thumb down, and have your friend push your arm down; or, if you prefer, make a circle of your thumb and first finger of either hand—hold them tightly and have your friend pull them apart. If you are too strong for your friend, then use a weaker finger.

Then experiment with different words, and see how negative words weaken you, while positive words make you strong.

When words can have such a powerful effect on the physical body, is it any wonder that nobody wants to do business with a negative person?

Positive people are stronger, and they make those around them feel better physically.

Unpleasant thoughts produce unpleasant faces. This story says it best: Once when President Abraham Lincoln turned down a recommendation from his advisers to appoint a certain man to an important post, he explained that he didn't like the man's face.

"The man is not responsible for his face," the advisers objected.

"Every man past forty is responsible for his face," Lincoln replied.

If you want to have a pleasant, youthful face, remember to think positive thoughts.

BECOME STRONG IN BOTH DIMENSIONS

José Silva will cover some special alpha techniques a little later to help you build up energy for the success thoughts, and to banish the negative energy of fear that sometimes is so strong.

For now it is important to remember that you are dealing with two dimensions: the physical, and the mental. You must take steps to use both dimensions to help you reach your full potential.

You can learn your sales scripts perfectly, you can know the best attention getters, you can be the most persistent prospector on the staff, and you can master fifty closing techniques, but if you ignore the mental dimension you are still using only half your ability and you will achieve far less than half of your potential. If you don't get out and do something with your knowledge and ability, then you will achieve very little.

When you use all of your abilities, and you are persistent and professional, then you will achieve results that you will be proud of and other people will admire. And more importantly, you will earn a lot of money so you can have the things you want in your life, and can take care of your family the way you want to.

POWERFUL WORDS THAT SELL

Here are some positive words that will help you to make more sales:

Achieve, advantage, agree, beauty, benefit, character, charming, determined, fun, good, health, helpful, hope, ideal, industrious, investment (rather than cost), joy, kind, lovely, maximum, music, opportunity, pleasant, productive, rejoice, reliable, satisfy, save, smile, success, truth, unity, valuable, victory, you.

And here are some words to avoid:

Absurd, blame, can't, careless, complain, condemn, coward, crazy, crooked, die, don't, doubt, dummy, error, failure, fear, guilty, hard, hate, have to, hopeless, humiliate, hurt, if (not "if you do" but "when you do"), inferior, insane, jealousy, kill, liar, need, obstacle, pain, poor, poverty, scared, sick, stupid, tired, try, waste, won't, worry, wrong.

A salesperson is always a counselor. Good salespeople never sell anything; they introduce people to products or services. Good salespeople never mention cost; they never say, "It is going to *cost* you so much," or that you "have to pay" a certain amount. Customers know they must pay, that nothing is given away, free.

Just mention the quality of the product, the benefits to the customer. Then, when the customer is interested and you've got him in a position where he can use your product or service, tell him, "You only put up" a certain amount.

"Nobody wants a product to cost anything," José Silva adds. "They want it to be free. And remember, you don't have to tell people what they have to do. They don't have to do anything.

"Phrases like 'have to' and 'the cost is . . . ' and 'your price . . . ' should never be mentioned."

José Luis Romero, who works at Silva International Headquarters in Laredo, suggests to Silva Method lecturers that when they mention the price of the program, they say, "Your investment is . . . " When people make an investment, it is for their benefit.

Now here is another alpha exercise from José Silva:

LEARNING TO USE THE ALPHA LEVEL CONSCIOUSLY

When you attend the Silva Method Basic Lecture Series, you learn to enter the alpha level and function there with just one day of training. However, learning on your own takes longer. To be sure you learn to reach the alpha level on your own, I am going to ask you to invest forty days. After that, you will be ready to program yourself for whatever you desire.

When you enter sleep you enter alpha. But you quickly go right through alpha to the deeper levels of theta and delta.

Throughout the night your brain moves back and forth through alpha, theta, and delta, like the ebb and flow of the tide. These cycles last about ninety minutes.

In the morning, as you exit sleep, you come out through alpha, back into the faster beta frequencies that are associated with the outer conscious levels.

Some authors advise that as you go to sleep at night, you think about your goals. That way, you get a little bit of alpha time for programming. The only trouble is, you have a tendency to fall asleep.

For now, I just want you to practice a simple exercise

that will help you learn to enter and stay at the alpha level. Then in forty days, you will be ready to begin your programming.

In the meantime I will give you some additional tasks that you can perform at the beta level, that will help you prepare yourself so that you will be able to program more effectively at the alpha level when you are ready at the completion of the forty days.

Here is your alpha exercise:

You will practice this alpha exercise in the morning when you first wake up. Since your brain is starting to shift from alpha to beta when you first wake up, you will not have a tendency to fall asleep as you enter alpha.

Here are the steps to take:

1. *When you awake tomorrow morning, go to the bathroom if you have to, then go back to bed. Set your alarm clock to ring in fifteen minutes, just in case you do fall asleep again.*
2. *Close your eyes and turn them slightly upward toward your eyebrows (about 20 degrees). Research shows that this produces more alpha.*
3. *Count back slowly from 100 to 1. Do this silently. Wait about one second between numbers.*
4. *When you reach the count of 1, hold a mental picture of yourself as a success. An easy way to do this is to recall the most recent time when you were 100 percent successful. Recall the setting, what the scene looked like, and recall what you felt like.*
5. *Repeat mentally, "Every day in every way I am getting better, better, and better."*
6. *Then say to yourself, "I am going to count from 1 to 5; when I reach the count of 5, I will open my eyes, feeling fine and in perfect health, feeling better than before."*
7. *Begin to count. When you reach 3, repeat, "When I reach the count of 5, I will open my eyes, feeling fine and in perfect health, feeling better than before."*
8. *Continue your count to 4 and 5. At the count of 5,*

open your eyes and affirm mentally, "I am wide awake, feeling fine and in perfect health, feeling better than before. And this is so."

THESE EIGHT STEPS ARE REALLY ONLY THREE

Go over each of these eight steps so that you understand the purpose while at the same time becoming more familiar with the sequence.

1. *The mind cannot relax deeply if the body is not relaxed. It is better to go to the bathroom and permit your body to enjoy full comfort. Also, when you first awake, you may not be fully awake. Going to the bathroom ensures your being fully awake. But, in case you are still not awake enough to stay awake, set your alarm clock to ring in about fifteen minutes so you do not risk being late on your daily schedule.*

2. *Research has shown that when a person turns the eyes up about 20 degrees, it triggers more alpha rhythm in the brain and also causes more right brain activity. Later when we do our mental picturing it will be with our eyes turned upward at this angle. Meanwhile, it is a simple way to encourage alpha. You might want to think of the way you look up at the screen in a movie theater.*

3. *Counting backward is relaxing. Counting forward is activating. 1, 2, 3 is like "get ready, get set, go!" Three to 1 is pacifying. You are going nowhere except deeper within yourself.*

4. *Imagining yourself the way you want to be—while relaxed— creates the picture. Failures who relax and imagine themselves losing the sale frequently create a mental attitude that brings about failure. You will do the opposite. Your mental picture is one of success, and will create what you desire: Success.*

5. *Words repeated mentally—while relaxed—create the concepts they stand for. Pictures and words program the mind to make it so.*

6, 7 & 8. *These last three steps are simply counting to 5 to end your session. Counting up activates you. But it is still good to give yourself "orders" to become activated at the count of 5. Do this before you begin to count; do it again along the way; do it again as you open your eyes at 5.*

Once you wake up tomorrow morning and prepare yourself for this exercise, it all works down to three steps:

With your eyes turned upward twenty degrees—

A. *Count backwards from 100 to 1.*

B. *Mentally picture yourself successful and affirm your continuing success.*

C. *Count yourself out 1 to 5, affirming good health and wideawakeness.*

FORTY DAYS THAT CAN CHANGE YOUR LIFE . . . FOR THE BETTER

You know what to do tomorrow morning, but what about after that?

Here is the program:

• *Count backward from 100 to 1 for ten mornings.*
• *Count backward from 50 to 1 for ten mornings.*
• *Count backward from 25 to 1 for ten mornings.*
• *Count backward from 10 to 1 for ten mornings.*

After these forty mornings of countdown relaxation practice, count backward only from 5 to 1 and begin to use your alpha level.

People have a tendency to be impatient, to want to move faster. Please resist this temptation and follow my instructions as written. You must develop and acquire the ability to function consciously at alpha before the mental techniques will work properly for you. We've been researching in this field since 1944, longer than anyone else, and the techniques we have developed have helped millions of people worldwide to enjoy greater success and happiness, so please follow these simple instructions.

We are including a couple of items to help you:

At the end of this chapter and the next three are forms so that you can keep track of your practice sessions. Check off each time you practice the countdown, and as soon as you have done the required number, move on to the next exercise.

In addition, we are including other activities that you can practice during each ten-day period. This practice will help you develop skills that will be beneficial to you immediately.

MENTAL HOUSECLEANING

In addition to practicing the alpha technique Mr. Silva just gave you, you can also develop the skill we term ''Mental Housecleaning.''

During the day, practice Mental Housecleaning. In the evening, before you go to bed, review and see how well you did. Ten days of practice will be a very big aid in helping you become a more positive thinker.

This is extremely important to learn before you advance too far with your alpha functioning. Thoughts are much more powerful at the alpha level, so you want to be sure that you have developed the habit of positive thinking. When you are functioning at the alpha level, you want positive thinking to be automatic.

Here is what to do:

You recall from our previous discussion that positive thinking is thinking about what you want, rather than what you don't want.

During the day, notice what you think about, and notice what you say.

Do you imagine yourself having a difficult time getting appointments, or do you imagine yourself making presentations to a lot of people?

Here are some words and phrases that you want to eliminate from your vocabulary:

Negative	Positive
I can't . . .	I can . . .
That makes me sick	I dislike that
I don't think so	I think . . .
I forgot . . .	It slipped my mind
I'm a failure	I'm getting there
I'm shy	I'm assertive
This person is going to say No	How I can help this person?

Here is what to do when you notice that you are using negative words and phrases:

Stop, and cancel out the negative words by saying, "Cancel-cancel." Then replace the negative words with positive words.

It is very important to always finish with a positive statement, a positive thought.

A fifty-five-year-old man who attended the Silva Method training in Albuquerque, New Mexico, had this to say after reflecting on his language for a while: "For years I've used the phrases, 'I can't see that,' 'It's a pain in the neck,' and 'It's a pain in the . . . .' Well, I won't finish the phrase, but let me explain: I wear glasses, I have headaches in the back of my head, and I have hemorrhoids!"

That got a laugh from the other members of the seminar, but when a person has suffered with those problems for several decades, it is no joke.

BE GOOD TO YOURSELF AND BE MORE SUCCESSFUL

What do you think about:

- Do you think about a prospect saying No or do you think about them saying Yes?
- Do you think about the last rejection, or about helping your next customer select the best product?
- Do you worry about the way you said the wrong thing on your last call, or do you think about saying the right thing next time?

There are many ways that you can be more positive, when you think of things from the customer's point of view.

A SECRET WAY TO PROTECT YOURSELF FROM NEGATIVITY AND REJECTION

Sometimes you might find yourself in a situation where you cannot say "Cancel-cancel." For instance, what do you do if your sales manager or a customer says something negative to you? If you tell them "Cancel-cancel" they might just Cancel-cancel you!

Instead of that, just give them a big Zero. In a computer, the program uses either a Zero or a One—that is, the circuit is either open or closed. When it is open, nothings gets through.

So give the negative words a big Zero by saying, "Oh."

For example:

"You really fouled up this time!"

"Oh? Well, what can I do to make it right?"

By doing that, you are canceling out the negative thought, and replacing it with a positive thought.

These techniques work. Read what a giant New Jersey pharmaceutical manufacturing firm had to say after learning the Silva Method:

" 'Cancel-cancel' and 'better and better' are new phrases being spoken at (the pharmaceutical firm) after 150 employees participated in the Silva Method training.

"For over 150 employees, the phrase 'better and better' is synonymous with a new way of thinking, a philosophy of one's own inner consciousness, and a different attitude about life, work, and other people."

"Even though I went into the course with a certain amount of 'show me' attitude, I have to admit that I thoroughly enjoyed the program," a company merchandising director said. "It gave me a new sense of awareness about myself and the importance of working with fellow employees," he continued. "I am applying what I learned by trying to develop the ability to channel my interests and accomplishments so there is less wasted time and motion. The concept certainly makes you stop and think."

BE KIND TO YOURSELF

It takes time to learn any new skill. And positive thinking is a new skill. We have been programmed, biologically and by our parents and teachers, to watch out for trouble. This helps us to survive in the physical world, because there are many things in the world that have the potential to harm us.

Therefore, you might notice that you are using quite a few negative words during the day.

Some people become depressed when they discover this. They beat themselves up mentally and verbally: "Wow, am I negative! I can't even pass the first part of this course!"

We'd suggest a different approach.

Instead of looking at the downside—how many negative things you might be saying during the day—look at the good side. Or as somebody once put it, Look for the good and praise it.

Now what, you might ask, can be good about realizing that you are saying so many negative things?

The fact that you noticed it is good. Now that you are aware, you can take steps to change.

Once you begin to think and talk about the things you want rather than the things you don't want, you have opened a big door to success.

EVALUATE YOUR PROGRESS

You might be surprised just how much this one simple exercise—Mental Housecleaning—can help you. To get an idea of how much this can benefit you, do this:

Notice during the day how people respond to you as you use positive words and phrases instead of negative ones.

At night when you are ready to go to sleep, notice whether you feel better than you normally do, and if you go to sleep easier and faster than before.

In the morning when it is time to get up, notice whether you find it a little easier to get up and face the new days with its challenges and opportunities.

Record Book

This could be the *most important page* in this chapter. All superstar salespeople know the importance of keeping good records. You are a winner, and you will demonstrate it to yourself by recording your progress on this page.

Besides the countdowns, what is the most valuable technique you learned in Chapter 2? _____

How will this technique help you? _____

Why is this important to you? _____

Date used and results: _____

Practice Log:

Day 1   (100–1 countdown)   [ ]
Day 2   (100–1 countdown)   [ ]
Day 3   (100–1 countdown)   [ ]
Day 4   (100–1 countdown)   [ ]
Day 5   (100–1 countdown)   [ ]
Day 6   (100–1 countdown)   [ ]
Day 7   (100–1 countdown)   [ ]
Day 8   (100–1 countdown)   [ ]
Day 9   (100–1 countdown)   [ ]
Day 10   (100–1 countdown)   [ ]

Congratulations, you are now ready to go on to the 50–1 countdowns. Please turn to the last page of Chapter 3 and record your practice sessions there.

3

PROFESSIONALISM—LAW OF RATIOS

There was a man who loved chocolate chip cookies. He loved them so much that he purchased a chocolate chip cookie machine. The salesman told him it would make all the chocolate chip cookies he wanted.

He poured in the flour and other ingredients and of course a lot of chocolate chips, turned on the switch, and waited. Pretty soon the machine started to rumble and shake, then it got warm and steam started coming out of it. He could begin to smell the cookies baking, and pretty soon the conveyor belt started moving and sure enough, there came dozens of chocolate chip cookies.

For several days the machine turned out chocolate chip cookies, the best he had ever eaten.

Then one day it stopped.

"It must be stuck," he said. He hit it with his hand, but it did not start up again. He kicked it. Still nothing. "It must be broken," he concluded. "Well, it was nice while it lasted."

He never realized that the reason the machine did not give him any more chocolate chip cookies was because he had not put any more ingredients into the machine. The cause-and-effect formula applies, even to chocolate chip cookie machines.

YOU CAN'T DEPOSIT WISHES AND GONNA-DOS IN THE BANK— THEY ARE NOT LEGAL TENDER

There's really no mystery about what it takes to be a successful salesperson: You must persuade people to purchase your product or service, and do it now. The more people you persuade, the more successful you are.

That sounds simple. The difficulty comes in knowing *how* to go about doing it. Everybody knows *what* it takes, but not everybody knows *how* to do it.

The good news is, you can learn how.

Let's take a look at how to go about persuading a lot of people to purchase your product or service.

First, you must find people who are willing to listen. A lot of people. Once you have that, you can learn how to tell your story more persuasively and more effectively: how to establish rapport, how to find out what your prospects really want, how to show how your product or service can help them get what they really desire, and how to understand what people's real objections are, and when they are just making excuses.

You can do all of this . . . once you have people to talk to. But, you must have people to talk to first.

THE BENCH IS WARM ENOUGH— NOW GET IN THE GAME

You can only make a sale when you call on prospects and tell them your story. Then why do salespeople hesitate to make calls?

Fear.

Fear of rejection.

We all want to belong, to be liked, to be accepted. It is part of our biological programming, our survival programming. The more friends we have, the better our chances of survival.

People who are controlled by this need for approval have a difficult time in sales, because they tend to avoid risking rejection. They hesitate to ask for appointments, and when they get appointments they hesitate to close and ask for the order . . . and the money.

Some people get a feeling of security by being in control of every situation. The trouble is, they hesitate to enter situations that they cannot control.

They also have difficulty in sales because they cannot establish rapport with their prospects. By trying to control everything, they do not let the prospect express his or her needs and wishes and apprehensions.

In order to become highly successful, you must make up your mind to take risks. You must develop strategies that permit you to risk rejection, that allow you to go into situations where you do not have absolute control. In this book, we will show you several ways to program yourself at the alpha level so that you will be comfortable in situations that used to make you apprehensive.

Here's some good news, a key to make you more successful: Selling is a numbers game.

The more people you tell your story to, the more sales you will make.

The more sales you make, the more money you will make. And in the game of selling, money is the way we keep score.

HOW A YOUNGSTER LEARNED TO LOVE MAKING COLD CALLS

A young would-be salesman learned to love making cold calls. Here is the story the way Burt Goldman, a Silva Method lecturer from California, tells it in the book *The Silva Mind Control Method of Mental Dynamics* (Pocket Books):

One day Roger G. phoned to report how effectively he had used the Silva Method to solve a problem involving his thirteen-year-old son Shawn. Shawn wanted to earn some extra money and had his father drop him off in a nearby neighborhood with a basket of stencils, paint, and brushes. Shawn was going to paint numbers on the curbs in front of houses. The numbers would make it easier to identify the address. Shawn would sell his service for one dollar.

Roger, a salesman, was easing his son into the profession. Even if Shawn did not take to sales, at least he would have a better idea of what his father did, and that was Roger's primary interest. He felt that this was an easy sell and that his son might even make a few dollars at it. Shawn, who had never tried anything like it before, was excited and could hardly wait to begin.

Roger dropped Shawn off in a residential neighborhood and promised to return within two hours. An hour and a half later Roger pulled up to the curb where Shawn sat, his chin resting on his fist, with a dejected look on his face that brightened when he realized he was being picked up.

Dropping his basket on the floor of the car with a bang, he sat heavily on the backseat and sighed. "Boy, Dad, I don't know how you do it. That was the worst experience I've ever had in my whole life. I don't ever want to do that again."

Needless to say, his father was disappointed. He asked, "What happened, Shawn? Didn't anybody buy the service?"

"Oh yeah," replied his son, "a few people paid me a dollar to paint their numbers on the curb. It was the ones who slammed the door in my face that bothered me." And shaking his head he asked again, "How do you do it, Dad? How can you take that?"

"Take what? What are you talking about, son?" Roger asked.

"You know what I mean. People are so nasty. They cursed me, and threw me out of their houses. Some of them yelled at me. I didn't realize that people were so mean."

On questioning, it turned out that none of these things were really happening, although Shawn thought that they were. He had faced, for the first time in his life, the bane of the sales profession, rejection. At age thirteen he had never gotten so much of it in so short a period of time. Everyone, it seemed to him, rejected him—which to him meant that they didn't like him. It was too much; he couldn't handle it and would never expose himself to that experience again. "Well, did you sell any?" his father asked.

Shawn reached into his pocket and pulled out a crinkled dollar bill, and then a few more until he had accumulated a small pile. His father's eyes opened a bit wider as he asked, "How much is there?"

Shawn counted and said, "Six dollars."

"Six dollars!" his father exclaimed. "But Shawn, that's terrific. You were only out for a hour and a half and you made six dollars. I think that's pretty good."

"No, it's not" was the reply. "I'm not going out there again, I hate it. I'd rather do anything than knock on doors again."

"How many people did you call on, Shawn?" his father asked.

"About a thousand."

His father shook his head seriously and said, "Shawn, you must be mistaken. You weren't out long enough to call on a thousand people."

"Well then, maybe fifty or sixty," he said after thinking about it for a moment.

"You know, Shawn," his father began, "if you called on sixty people and made six dollars that means you sold ten percent of them. That's a pretty good average." Shawn's features took on the look of total misery at that statement, and his father chuckled and quickly added, "It's okay, son, I'm not going to make you go out anymore." He shrugged and continued, "At least you know what it's all about now."

Roger reported that here was a good test case for the changing of a viewpoint for him to use. Shawn had a neg-

ative attitude toward selling that Roger was going to turn
around so that his son would have a positive attitude and
taste success.

Shawn was a recent graduate of the Silva children's
class, and he had seen some spectacular events take place
at the seminar for youngsters. He had been a participant in
many of them, so what Roger said did not seem at all
strange to him.

"Shawn," his father asked, "how would you like me to
put a spell on you so that every time you knock on a door,
the person answering will pay you a dollar to paint the
house number on the curb?"

"Every one of them?" Shawn asked.

"Every one," Roger answered.

"Sure."

For it wasn't selling he feared; it was the rejection. If it
could be guaranteed that he would make a sale in every
house, then he did not have to fear rejection. The most
timid salesperson in the world would have the courage of
a tiger if every call were guaranteed to result in a sale.

Thirteen-year-old Shawn G. stood outside the car while
Roger put the spell on him. Pointing his index finger at
Shawn's chest, Roger quickly moved his arm to describe a
five-pointed star in the air, finishing with a dot in the center
of the star at a nice flourish, while Shawn stood with his
chest out as though catching the symbol.

"That's it," Roger said.

"Now let me get this straight," Shawn said. "Every person I call on will buy?"

"Yes," Roger said. Shawn grabbed his basket of paint
and started off. "Wait a minute," his father cried. Back
Shawn came to hear what more he had to say. "You know,
Shawn," Roger said, "on second thought it wouldn't be
fair if you were to sell every one. Have you ever heard me
speak about paying your dues?"

He had, and he understood that if it was too easy it might
hurt his growth and that he had to take a few knocks just
so he could experience what people with less resources had
to experience.

"Well," Roger said, "this is the way the spell is going to work. You call on fifty people. The first forty-five will say no. The next five will all buy. Can you handle that?"

"Sure," Shawn said, "but I'm going to get past them as quickly as I can."

"That's all right," Roger replied, "so long as you knock on fifty doors. But Shawn," he continued, "I really don't have complete control over this spell. Some of the five might slip into the forty-five, so here." Handing him a piece of paper and a pencil, he said, "Every time you speak to a person, make a mark here so that you can keep score, and if one of the five slips in and you accidentally sell them, circle the mark. When you get to number forty-five, if two people have bought, then only the next three will buy."

Off he went, skeptical but game. Roger left to have a cup of coffee and returned about an hour later. Shawn was walking briskly down the street, paint all over his pants. When he noticed his father he waved and Roger pulled over.

"Wow!" he exclaimed. "That spell really works, I'm selling like crazy. Dad, how about leaving me here, I'll take a bus back. I don't want to quit just yet, there's plenty of paint left in the can and I have the rest of the next block to work."

Roger told the story just as it happened. The method worked; his son's viewpoint changed. The first time he knocked on doors, every door was a potential rejection. Shawn hated that. He hated the feeling that his finger on the doorbell or his knuckles knocking on the door would bring a person who rejected him. He couldn't deal with that for very long.

But after the so-called spell, which you might liken to the placebo effect because Shawn believed that the spell was going to influence the people he called on, everything changed. Forty-five people were going to say no. That's not rejection. That's just a job to do, to get past those forty-five as quickly as possible so he could get to the five who were going to buy.

As long as he believed that, he could be a tiger. He not

only didn't care any longer if they slammed the door in his face, he welcomed it, and the quicker they did it the better. He would scratch off one more on his way to number forty-five.

Of course what was happening was that his enthusiasm and courage showed through and the percentage of his sales increased dramatically. More and more of the magic five slipped through. By the time he reached the forty-fifth person he was so involved with the spell that counting was no longer necessary and he began to greet a resounding "No" with an "Oh boy, another one out of the way."

His viewpoint had been changed. Instead of seeing the door from a negative viewpoint (hate), he began to see it from a positive viewpoint (love), and that helped him to achieve his goal.

Incidentally, there is a postscript to the story. Roger had inadvertently created a monster. Shawn's introduction to sales took place during summer vacation, and it wasn't long before he was making $200 a week and had two friends working for him. It took all of his father's power of persuasion to get him back into school at vacation's end.

Make the big switch from hate to love, and you will enjoy life more. Then the affirmation "Every day, in every way, I'm getting better, better, and better" will truly take root and your life will indeed improve.

A FORMULA FOR MAKING MORE SALES

Successful salespeople make calls. They make a lot of calls, because they realize that above all else, selling is a numbers game.

If you want to make ten sales, and you know what percentage you sell when you make your presentation, then it is very easy to figure out how many calls you must make to make your ten sales.

If you sell one person in ten, then you must ask one hundred people to buy in order to make ten sales.

So your very first task is to get off the bench and get into the game. Even if you are not a very good player, it is still necessary for you to get into the game.

Once you are in the game, then you can improve your skills. You can learn to increase your percentage. You can learn to sell one out of ten, one out of eight, one out of five. Some days you might sell to every person you talk to, and some days you might not sell anything. Some of the five might slip in, and in some instances, they might slip over into the next fifty!

The law of averages will work in the long run. When you make enough calls, you will make enough sales, and reap the rewards of success.

HOW A "BAD" SALESMAN SELLS $1 MILLION A YEAR

Dave Bellizzi has a perfect example of how the numbers game can make you rich:

"When I first started selling insurance," he recalled, "my sales manager pointed out one man to me and told me that he had the worst approach and worst sales pitch he had ever heard. And he added that this guy was one of the top salesmen in the company. Every year, his sales were well over $1 million.

"I asked the sales manager how this could be. 'Go listen to him and find out,' he told me. So I did.

"The guy would dial a number out of the phone book. When somebody would answer, he'd say, 'You don't want to buy any insurance today, do you?' That's awful, a completely negative approach. Most people would answer 'No' and hang up. This guy just kept calling, dialing one number after another.

"Maybe one person out of a hundred would say 'Yes.' The thing was, that person would buy. The guy sold insurance to almost everybody he got an appointment with.

"Why were his sales so high every year? Because he

was calling 300 people a day, six days a week. That's 1,800 calls every week. Only eighteen would listen to him, and some of those people had medical problems and would get turned down, but he sold enough insurance to make the Million Dollar Club.

"Then one day, he learned about asking for referrals," Bellizzi added, "and he increased his sales significantly. He used the same approach: 'You don't have any friends who want to buy insurance, do you?' Can you imagine how much he could have sold if he had a better approach? The Theory of Ratios always works."

PEOPLE REMEMBER YOUR SUCCESSES

Isn't it interesting how we tend to remember our failures, while other people usually remember our successes?

Do you remember the people who fail? Take a little test:

Who is the baseball player who is known as the Home Run King, the player who dominated the sport for more than twenty years and made the New York Yankees the best team in baseball?

Almost everybody knows we mean Babe Ruth.

Babe Ruth hit 714 home runs in his career. There are legends about his great ability.

Now let's take the other side of that coin.

Do you remember the name of the major league baseball player who holds the record for the most strikeouts?

Who was the player who struck out more times than anybody else in the history of the game?

Very few people know that the player who had the most strikeouts in his career was . . . Babe Ruth.

That's right, he struck out more than 1,300 times, almost double the number of times he hit home runs.

What do people remember about Babe Ruth?

Do you think he would have been the home run king if he had been so afraid of striking out that he hesitated to swing at the ball?

Somebody pointed out that ships are safe when they are in the harbor; but ships aren't built to stay in the harbor.

Set sail toward your goal.

Get in the game and start swinging.

You will never know whether you will wind up the strikeout king, or the home run king, or both—like the salesman Dave Bellizzi just told about—until you start.

HOW TO PROGRAM YOURSELF TO GET OFF THE BENCH AND GET INTO THE GAME

How can you program yourself to make more calls?

First, use young Shawn's story as an example to help you cope with the fear of rejection.

In the morning, as you finish your 100 to 1 countdown, mentally picture yourself making calls and enjoying it. Each time someone turns you down, imagine making a deposit in the bank; you are paying your dues, you are making an investment that will pay you big dividends in the future.

Remember Mental Housecleaning. Always "Look for the good and praise it." After every call, figure out all of the things you did right. Did you last a little longer than you did on the previous call? If so, figure out what you did to keep you in the game longer this time.

While at your level in the morning, review your reasons for wanting to make calls. How will it help you to make more calls? It will help you because you will make more sales, which means that you will earn more money.

Most people, when they think of earning more money, usually have it mentally earmarked for a particular purpose, and you probably do too. What is that purpose? Why do you want more money?

Is it for your retirement? To provide nice things for your family? For your children's education?

What will you use that money for?

When you answer that question, you have your motivation.

THE GOLD IS THERE FOR THE TAKING

In order to help you to better understand the numbers game as it relates to prospecting, imagine two people who have come to the goldfields to make their fortunes.

The first day the foreman shows each of them a large pile of sand and a sluice box (a sluice box is a device for separating the gold from the sand). Then he tells each of them that if they shovel the whole pile of sand through the sluice box, they will each average about $300 worth of gold a day.

The first person goes to work shoveling the sand through the box. The second is much too smart for that. He's not going to do all that unnecessary work. He is going to poke his fingers through the sand and just "pick out" the gold here and there. None of that hard work for him. He thinks he can tell which spots are most likely to contain gold.

Sure enough, he finds a gold nugget right off. So instead of shoveling all the sand, he keeps looking for nuggets. Maybe there is a nugget here. Maybe there. But most of the sand goes unchecked.

At the end of the day, when the first miner is shoveling the last of his pile of sand through the box and is ready to collect his $300, the second (hopefully) is realizing his mistake. He has done a halfway job, found only a few small nuggets, and made only $50.

The mistake was in trying to make money on every attempt. Selling and gold mining just don't work that way. It is the salespeople and the miners who are "dumb enough" to work hard and send enough raw material through the system who achieve their goals.

You never know where you'll strike gold, which shovelful of sand will contain a fortune. You'll never know which prospect will buy. You'll never know in advance when the magic spell will take effect.

So, make up your mind to play the numbers game, make

calls, as many calls as you possibly can. Remind yourself why you are making the calls; remind yourself of what your ultimate goal is . . . what you are going to buy with that money, and why that's important to you. Get in the game!

A STORY OF COURAGE

How would you like to work in a business where you are automatically rejected by everyone you call on?

That's what Lyn McKenzie did.

To make matters worse, she had never sold anything in her life. She had always been a housewife. Then a crippling illness put her in a wheelchair. And then her husband died, leaving her with a house but little money.

While other people might see many reasons for not even trying, Lyn McKenzie picked herself up, went out on her own, and started knocking on doors to raise money to begin a service to help handicapped people. Her story is one of the most courageous in this book.

Dr. Richard E. McKenzie was a psychologist. After serving as an Army Air Force pilot in World War II, he spent many years as Chief of the Stress and Fatigue Section at the USAF School of Aerospace Medicine. He worked with astronauts, teaching them stress-reduction techniques. After retiring from the Air Force, the McKenzies moved to San Antonio, Texas, where he eventually opened a private practice.

For many years, Dr. McKenzie was a scientific research consultant to Silva International. He and Lyn practiced the Silva Method techniques regularly. Dr. McKenzie wrote in his book *The Secret Place*, published by the Institute of Psychorientology, Inc., that they enjoyed living on their "ranchette" along with "some Peruvian Paso horses, some wonderful nondescript dogs and 'other things' that sting, bite or crawl."

In March of 1988, Lyn was stricken with a disease where the body's immune system malfunctions and damages the nerves. "The nerves get chewed up by your immune system, and signals cannot get through to give your legs the proper messages," she explained.

In August of that year, Dr. McKenzic brought his wife to the Silva Method International Convention in a wheelchair. They were programming and fighting back, using all of the Silva Method holistic faith-healing techniques. But the disease defied diagnosis. It resembled multiple sclerosis, but it wasn't.

At the Silva Convention in Laredo, a lot of people programmed for Lyn. "That was incredible energy," she said, "incredible energy."

The McKenzies continued to program and she was walking again a month later. Then tragedy struck again when her husband suddenly died.

Lyn didn't quit. She began planning what to do with the rest of her life.

She achieved one goal in August of 1989 when she attended the annual Silva Method International Convention to thank everybody for their help and to demonstrate her recovery to them by dancing at the Awards Dance.

The events of the previous year had made Lyn aware of a serious problem that needed to be corrected. Handicapped people are often left out of social activities. At the 1988 Awards Dance Lyn could only sit and watch as well-wishers expressed their sympathy. In 1989 she could participate, which was infinitely better.

Then she learned about a service, headquartered in Washington, D.C., called DateABLE, which gets handicapped people together socially.

She decided to organize the service in San Antonio. It would take a lot of money to get it going, which meant that she needed donations and grants from businesses, corporations, private agencies, the government . . . anybody who could help.

"I never did any selling before," Lyn said. But she knew that if it was going to happen, she was the one who had to do it.

"I knew I would give it my best shot. If it was going to

go, it definitely would be because of the energy and input I would put into it.''

It was difficult. She had no track to run on, no sales manager to give her advice and encouragement, to motivate her and push her out the door.

"When one is asking businesses for favors and donations," she said, "they get complete rejection. Very rarely do you come upon someone who says, 'Oh, yes, I'll be glad to do that.' Even when it's a worthwhile organization, it is very difficult.

"I knew that the rejection was not personal," she continued. "I knew that it was just a business answer. It did not mean that Lyn McKenzie was a nerd. It just meant that, 'Things are rough, and nobody has the money.' '' She didn't realize that the ''No money left in the budget'' answer was just an excuse.

"I have since found out that on the first contact you have with people, it is an impossible time to get any money because they don't know you, don't know if you are legitimate," she explained. "The money is really there. It is just that people are squeamish about giving it to an organization that they don't know anything about. But after they become comfortable with the fact that you *are* a viable organization, they are not so hesitant.

"So I just had to work on making the organization visible and very dependable, one that is aboveboard in all matters."

Lyn had two very important things going for her that helped her through the hard times:

- She had a lot of confidence in her ability to achieve whatever she set out to do, the kind of confidence that you get only from the successes that you have.
- She had a very strong desire to help the handicapped people she was doing this for.

"I always believed in myself," she said. "I always believed in the organization and what we could do. That feeling never faltered. I always had it."

Her hard work and belief paid off. She got the funding and everything else she needed to make her dream come true.

There was still another challenge that she still had, and still faces today: the malfunctioning immune system.

"My immune system is working correctly now," she said, "as long as I don't get over tired.

"When I get extremely tired, it stops, it absolutely stops working.

"I try to keep myself relaxed all the time. I like to be aware that I could get stressed out if I'm not careful. So I'm constantly aware, and try to keep my mind free of worry, free of any extraneous thought. Focusing my mind with all the things I have to do is very difficult," she said. "I keep myself from getting too tired. I know what I will be doing, so I pace myself, so that I don't have to go through that nonworking phase."

She is so busy that she seldom has time to go to her level during the day. "When I do have time for meditation," she said, "I have deep ones, and wonderful ones. On weekends I do wonderful programming. I am of the belief that that has given me enough energy to carry on through the busy week, when I don't have time to stop and go to my level."

José Silva says that when a person has had as much practice and success as Lyn McKenzie has, then all they need to do is to recall the feeling of being at alpha, and they will receive many of the same benefits again.

Whatever Lyn is doing is evidently enough. "I keep myself very healthy," she said. "I never get sick, not even a cold. I keep myself in such deep alpha at all times that I'm able to keep my immune system strong at all times."

She keeps DateABLE strong, too, to the benefit of a lot of wonderful people who have made new friends because of Lyn McKenzie.

GETTING ANY PROSPECT'S UNDIVIDED ATTENTION

The first thing you have to do when you call a prospect is to get their attention. You have to break through their veil of preoccupation and get them to notice you.

Some salespersons try to get noticed by wearing flashy clothing, telling jokes, handing out trinkets, putting on a show. These tactics work for some people, in some lines.

Regardless of what other strategies you use or how good you are at showmanship, you need to develop a good attention getter. You need a good opening line that will get your prospect's attention.

What could be better than offering them something they want?

"Would you like to make a million dollars?"

Most people would like to have a million dollars, and most people would be suspicious of that line. So, your attention getter also has to be credible. It also has to talk to them in terms of their interests.

THE PROFESSIONAL WAY TO APPROACH PEOPLE

Here are some ways that you can approach people to ask for an appointment.

1. Walk up to your prospect and say, "Mr. Prospect, how would you like to (mention a benefit of your product)?" If the prospect says Yes, set up an appointment to make your presentation. We'll show you how in a moment.
2. Walk up to Ms. Prospect and say, "Ms. Prospect, if I can show you a new way to do (mention a benefit of your product) would you be interested?" If the

answer is Yes, set up an appointment.
3. Walk up and say, "Mr. Prospect, if there were a new way to (mention a benefit of your product), you'd probably like to know more about that, wouldn't you?" Then set up the appointment.

The secret to getting appointments is to tell your prospect, within five seconds, what benefit he or she will receive in return for taking some of their valuable time to listen to you. If you have something new and interesting to say, they will listen to you.

You notice that each of the approaches mentioned above says the same thing, but in different ways. Which way would be the most effective way for someone to get an appointment with you?

A PROVEN WAY TO MAKE MORE APPOINTMENTS

Here is a professional way to make appointments, that has been proven in the field for more than twenty-five years. It works.

"Mr. Prospect, my name is (give your name). I'm with (identify your company). I know you're busy, but I stopped by because I'd like to show you a new idea, that's been of help to other (mention prospect's occupation), to help (mention a benefit of your product). Can I see you next Tuesday at 10:00, or would 2:30 be better?"

Here is how we might approach you: "Mr. Salesman, my name is Ed Bernd. I'm with the Silva Method of Mind Development. I know you're busy, but I stopped by because I'd like to show you a new idea, that's been of help to other salespeople, to help you dramatically increase your sales now. Can I see you next Tuesday at 10:00, or would 2:30 be better?"

Notice the various parts of this approach:

- First you identify yourself and your company. Many people have been taught to avoid talking to strangers, so introduce yourself.
- "I know you're busy . . . " Acknowledge that their time is valuable. People like and appreciate that: customer consciousness.
- " . . . stopped by to show you a new idea . . . " People like to see new things. Remember Show and Tell when you were in school? "New" is a powerful word, which is why it is used in advertising so frequently. Everybody wants to know what's new. Curiosity killed the cat. People are curious by nature—take advantage of it.
- " . . . that's been of help to other (mention prospect's occupation) . . . " People think that their situation is different from other people's, and they always want to know what's happening in their profession.
- " . . . to help you (mention a benefit)." People buy benefits. The first three questions that virtually every person has when you approach them are: (1) What's in it for me? (2) What's in it for me? (3) What's . . . Well, you know the rest. We will discuss benefits in detail in Chapters 10 and 11.
- "Can I see you next Tuesday at 10:00, or would 2:30 be better?" Give them two alternatives. "Do you want to meet with me, or do you want to meet with me?" Multiple choice is easier than answering an open ended (essay) question.

GETTING GOOD APPOINTMENTS BY PHONE

You can use the same approach to make appointments by telephone. Insert "called" in place of "stopped by."

Here are some tips for using the telephone:

Immediately show people the courtesy of asking if they have a moment to speak. "Mr. Prospect, my name is Ed Bernd. I'm with the Silva Method. Do you have a moment to talk?'' Very few people extend this courtesy. They will be surprised and appreciative when you do. Most will let you continue. If someone is busy and tells you, then simply ask when it would be convenient to call back. They will tell you. And when you call back, they will be willing to listen to you because you were considerate of their time. They will feel that they owe you a couple of minutes of their time.

When you talk on the phone, talk slowly. Fast talking may indicate nervousness, lack of belief, a con job, no confidence. People like to listen to a slow, smooth, confident voice. Tape yourself when you are on the phone and listen to the tape played back. How would you react to your voice?

Stand up when you are talking on the telephone. Professional announcers know that standing up helps you to project more authority, more power.

Get a shoulder rest or headset so you do not tire yourself by having to hold the receiver in your hand for long periods of time.

AN EASY WAY TO PRACTICE

Jeff Slutsky has a unique way of developing "benefit statements" to get people's attention.

"When people ask me what business I'm in," Slutsky said, "I like to give them an answer that will cause them to say, 'No kidding! How do you do that?'

"For instance," he continued, "my brother Marc and I don't say that we do seminars on marketing, sales, and advertising. We say, 'We teach people how to advertise and promote so that they can increase sales without spending any money.' That jumps out and grabs them! When a person responds, 'How do you do that?' they are basically asking us to give them a sales presentation.''

Slutsky is a Silva Method graduate, and uses his level to help him develop the benefit statements that will cause people to ask, "How do you do that?"

An insurance salesman was having trouble getting appointments to tell people about a retirement program. Slutsky helped him develop this benefit statement: "We specialize in helping our clients accumulate a million dollars for retirement without having to contribute too much on a monthly basis." People respond, "You're kidding—how do you do that?" The salesman then says, "Let's set up a time and get together, so I can show you."

"It takes some time and some real thought to come up with a good one," Slutsky said. "You have to get a different one for each specific product line or service line that you sell. They really come in handy when you start to introduce yourself to people."

To develop your own benefit statements, Slutsky says you must have some quiet time at your level. "If you force yourself to concentrate, it's not going to work," he explained. "It is one of those things where you work on it, then sort of put it away and a few days later it will come to you. You have to know what you are looking for, and then give your brain time to bring the solution up from the subconscious to the conscious."

Our benefit statement for the Silva Method is: "We show people how to actually use the untapped power of their mind to help them easily get whatever they want in life." People say, "No kidding, how do you do that?"

The Slutsky brothers have an interesting way of testing their benefit statements to see if they work as well as expected: They try them out at cocktail parties, or other social settings. At a social gathering it is natural for people to ask what you do for a living. When you tell them and they answer, "No kidding, how do you do that?" then you know you have a good benefit statement.

The brothers explain many of their techniques in their book *Streetfighting* (Prentice-Hall, 1984).

YOU CAN DO IT WHEN YOU SET YOUR MIND TO IT

Everyone can learn to sell. It takes determination, and persistence. And you can program yourself for that. Just remember to think about your goal, what you want, how it will change your life, and why that is important to you.

Linda Almaraz, a realtor in Oklahoma City, learned how. "I started off in life by failing the first grade," she said. "Now, that's pretty bad. I got through school on my personality, because I thought I wasn't smart."

She got a job working in physical fitness as an instructress. Then someone offered her a job in selling and management for a beauty and health-care salon. She figured her personality would help her get by in that job.

"But there was a catch," she said. "The lady who hired me said that I had to take a course. She said that she would pay for it, but I had to take it if I was going to work for her. So I agreed. It was the Silva Method."

Through these jobs, Linda learned about personal grooming, and she got her body into shape so that she had the energy to pursue her dream: to become one of the top salespeople in Oklahoma.

She did just that, with the help of the Silva Method techniques. And you can too!

"When I started selling," she recalled, "I said that I was not going to be known like other realtors. I was going to be known for my professionalism, my caring, my willingness to help other people . . . and make a lot of money."

At the alpha level, she programmed all of those traits. She got the message through to Willie.

"Within two years, I got an award as Most Cooperative Realtor of the Year." Once again, mental techniques, which rely on cooperation, carried the day.

"They had not issued this award for ten years," she added. "It stated that it was granted to someone who showed professionalism, fairness . . . all my dreams were coming true, strictly from visualization.

"That award listed all the things I had programmed that I would be, two years before.

"I use the Silva Method techniques to make money, to make friends, and to gather knowledge."

Even though she had thought she was not smart, and had gotten through school on her personality, she found out otherwise.

"It's been amazing that all of the dreams that I had as a little girl, the Silva Method was the vehicle of getting there.

"Everyone has dreams that, 'One day I will do this . . . but I don't know how to get there.' Silva opened up my mind," she said. "The best part is that you do it for the highest good. I wouldn't trade it for anything."

YOUR CURRENT ASSIGNMENT

After completing your first ten days of practice, you are ready for your next assignment:

Continuing to practice your mental exercise, but shorten the countdown to 50 to 1. Otherwise, continue the same as before. When you have checked off all ten days on the form at the end of this chapter, you are ready to proceed to the next phase.

After you have practiced Mental Housecleaning for ten days, and are satisfied with your results, you can add a new practice to your daily routine.

Of course, continue to practice Mental Housecleaning from now on.

Your new assignment is to make appointments. Set yourself a daily goal, and make a certain number of appointments each day.

For now, set a goal that is comfortable for you, and meet or exceed that goal.

Make up your mind to approach at least ten people a

day, and ask for appointments. If you are already calling that many people a day, then increase what you are doing by 10 percent. And make sure you follow through and call that number of people every single day.

Record Book

This could be the *most important page* in this chapter. All superstar salespeople know the importance of keeping good records. You are a winner, and you will demonstrate it to yourself by recording your progress on this page.

Besides the countdowns, what is the most valuable technique you learned in Chapter 3? _____

How will this technique help you? _____

Why is this important to you? _____

Date used and results: _____

Practice Log:

Day 1 (50–1 countdown) [ ]
Day 2 (50–1 countdown) [ ]
Day 3 (50–1 countdown) [ ]
Day 4 (50–1 countdown) [ ]
Day 5 (50–1 countdown) [ ]
Day 6 (50–1 countdown) [ ]
Day 7 (50–1 countdown) [ ]
Day 8 (50–1 countdown) [ ]
Day 9 (50–1 countdown) [ ]
Day 10 (50–1 countdown) [ ]

Congratulations, you are now ready to go on to the 25–1 countdowns. Please turn to the last page of Chapter 4 and record your practice sessions there.

4

IF I'D KNOWN WHERE I WAS GOING I'D HAVE TAKEN A SHORTCUT

Somebody once pointed out that if Columbus had turned back, nobody would have blamed him . . . but nobody would have remembered him either.

What kept ol' Chris sailing west toward the ends of the earth, when everybody else "knew" there was nothing there but an edge to fall off of?

Christopher Columbus had a plan. Sure, there was a major mistake in his plan, but that plan still led him on to bring glory to himself and riches to Spain that were even greater than he and Queen Isabella had imagined in their original plan.

HOW TO BE YOUR OWN BEST SALES MANAGER

How would you go about creating a plan that will keep you moving toward your goal?

Remember the story of Shawn in Chapter 2, whose father, Roger, created a sound management plan? If Shawn wanted to make five sales, he had to call on fifty people. If he wanted to make ten sales, he had to call on—well, you can figure it out.

Shawn knew what he wanted, and he knew how to get it. Anytime he wanted to, he could sit down and figure out how many doors he had to knock on in order to get the amount of money he desired.

And when he wanted more money than he could make himself, it was easy for Shawn to formulate a plan for hiring other people. He could simply extend his basic operation and make as much money as he needed.

HOW PAUL GRIVAS PLANNED HIS WAY TO SUCCESS

For several years, Paul Grivas was our Silva Method director in New York. In addition, he translated the Silva Method into Greek and introduced the Method in Greece.

How was Paul able to accomplish so much?

One of his secrets was his detailed planning. Just managing New York is a big enough job for most people. But Paul did that and also found time to translate the course into another language and then manage our operations in that country for several years in addition to his duties in New York. In his spare time, he even wrote a musical play!

"I keep records of everything," Paul told us. "When I run an advertisement in the newspaper, I keep track of the day it ran, which paper it ran in, which page it was on, the position on that page, the day of the week, the day of the month, which month, what the weather was that day— everything I can think of."

The ads invited people to a free introductory lecture about the Silva Method. Paul said that besides keeping records of how many people came to the intros and how many signed up, he kept other data also. He wanted to know what other activities were going on that night, what the weather was that night, what he said and how he said it, how many of the people at the intro already knew something about the Silva Method before he started to speak.

He also kept records of what benefits people were seeking when they came to the intro. There is a place for that on the back of the introductory lecture cards.

It is interesting that the Silva Method lecturers who keep the best records are the most successful at selling the program to a lot of people.

There is a special way to keep records if you want to reach your full potential.

Remember how we pointed out that Shawn would average five sales for every fifty people he spoke to, but that some of the five might slip over into the next fifty. There is a special way of keeping records that takes that into account, and you will learn it in just a moment.

EXPECTANCY VS. WISHING

The people who don't keep good records wait and wish that something good would happen. Wishing is the narcotic of the salespeople who don't know exactly what to do to accomplish their goal. They just wish that everything would turn out okay and they would "sell a lot."

"Boy, I'm really going to get 'em this month," they say, not knowing, (1) how many people they have to talk with to sell enough to accomplish their goal, (2) where they get their best results from, whether from new contacts, or referrals from satisfied customers, or (3) how many more contacts they would have to make to sell 25 percent more.

How valuable would it be to know exactly how many people you would need to talk to in order to reach your goal?

IGNORANCE DOESN'T PREVENT SUFFERING

If you are content not knowing what you need to do to reach your goal, then you don't need to keep good records. Anyway, seems like a lot of trouble.

Too much trouble? Ask the top salespeople. They keep

good records. They treat this seriously, like their career was on the line.

The losers in any company keep shabby records, and then only to keep the sales manager off their back. Ask losers what they have to do to sell 25 percent more and they can't tell you.

Ask them at 3 P.M. on the 14th day of the month if they are on target to reach their goals and they can't tell you. Ask them what the exact ratio of contacts to sales is, how many prospects they get from satisfied customers, and they don't know! Ask them where their next sale is coming from, and they don't know.

They just wish that they'd make more sales so they could reach their goals.

A wonderful management technique? No. There have been winners and losers in companies forever, and the winners keep better, more involved, more detailed records so that they will know two very important things:

Am I seeing enough people?

Is there a bottleneck somewhere that is impeding progress?

AN EFFECTIVE STRATEGY FOR MORE SUCCESS

The secret is in knowing what you have to do to reach your goal, and then making up your mind to DO IT!

In just a moment you will learn how to keep track of what you have to do to reach your goal. In a later chapter, we'll show you exactly how to use deep levels of mind to talk directly with Willie and motivate yourself to do what you have to do to succeed.

Right now, watch this math and you will learn how:

Records = Sales.

Let's say someone approached 180 people last month. They asked 90 to buy and sold 30 units which totaled $9,000. The process runs just like a factory. The raw material (180) gets refined (to 90), then refined again (to 30) which is the finished product.

You have 180 suspects = 90 prospects = 30 units = $9,000.

Little Johnny talks to 18 people about his apples, asks 9 people to buy, sells 3 and totals 90 cents. That's 18 people = 9 closes = 3 sales = $.90.

SIMPLE ARITHMETIC

Now here is a question for you: What would you tell little Johnny to do if he wants to earn a total of $1.80?

Any junior high school student can tell you the simple answer to that one. But ask most professional salespeople that question and listen to all the complicated, foggy explanations that you'll get.

And remember that the biggest, most foolish excuse that anyone in sales ever used for not seeing enough people:

"My business is different."

"MY BUSINESS IS DIFFERENT"

Yes, that's right, their business is different.

They somehow want the factory to produce the finished product without finding and refining raw materials.

Can you imagine the heads of an enormous factory standing outside and wondering why there isn't enough finished product coming out of their factory?

When you tell them there isn't enough raw material going in, they say, "Our business is different. We don't like to go out and find the raw material we need. We just like to keep wishing that somehow it will just show up."

Now, it's a very simple formula:

If you want to increase the last total, then increase the other numbers in the equation.

HERE'S HOW IT WORKS

Picture a large factory that processes raw materials into the finished product. Just like the factory that finds valuable raw material, refines it and makes it even more valuable, you can "find" raw material and process it into the finished product.

If there isn't enough finished product coming out, then you check to see if there is enough raw material going in. The raw material in this case would be the people you talk to about your product or service.

If there is enough raw material coming through the door, then you would look for the bottleneck and make the necessary adjustments in the process to get the desired quality and production levels.

ELIMINATING BOTTLENECKS

When you want to increase the production process in a sales business, you work on improving your selling skills.

Study more information on selling, then pick up the phone, dial a number, and tell somebody about your product or service. Use the new sales skills you want to develop, and learn how they work. This will improve your production process in your "factory."

Study other aspects of your "production" process: your customers, your referrals, your literature, etc.

FAILPROOF FORMULA

Once you have kept good records, you can set your goals with a failproof formula. If someone's goal is to sell 40 units for the month, they would usually set four weekly goals of 10.

If you look at anyone's records, you will see that they do not sell exactly 10 every week. There will be a high week, two medium weeks, and a low week.

So instead of setting your goals the same every week, set goals for one high week, two medium weeks, and one low week.

It would look something like this:

High, 16 sales.
Medium, 12 sales.
Medium, 12 sales.
Low, 4 sales.

Notice this comes to a total of 44 sales in a month, leaving you a cushion of 10 percent.

HOW TO KEEP YOUR MOTIVATION HIGH

Suppose you used that old formula of 10 sales each week, and you made 4 sales the first week. That would demoralize most people and start the month with a "failure."

But with the realistic system, you could mark off your low week, pat yourself on the back, and plan for your next week.

Suppose you sold 16 the first week. Under the old system, even the best of us would tend to take it easy the next week.

But with the realistic, more accurate system, you don't have to ride the emotional roller coaster of uneven sales production that the less organized person must endure.

The percentages are: High, 40 percent; Medium, 30 percent; Medium, 30 percent; Low, 10 percent.

Did you notice the 10 percent cushion? The whole system is designed to help build and maintain your feeling of success.

The same formula works when projecting annual goals. A quarter (of a year) would be High, Medium, Medium,

Low. Your goals should be high enough to push you, but realistic enough to be reachable.

Carolyn Deal of Greensboro, North Carolina, one of our most productive Silva Method lecturers, says that she gives herself permission to fail. "I don't judge the success of my business on one event," she explained. "I've had introductory lectures where nobody showed up." That's why she is more interested in looking at her long-term goals than in worrying about whether she reaches a short-term goal or not.

Let the results of your efforts guide you in establishing future goals. Wilfred might claim to be able to triple your sales this week, but remember that Wilfred lies a lot. If Willie doesn't believe it (if you don't believe it on the Willie level, deep within) then you are not likely to reach the goal.

It is best when projecting overall increases to raise them 10 percent at a time. This keeps you from setting goals that are unrealistic.

You must believe in how valuable this formula can be to you.

Who motivates the motivator?

Now you know. Your own records serve to motivate you and keep you moving toward your goals. You are the answer.

José Silva adds this bit of advice: Do not let your first failure destroy you, nor your first success ruin you. Recognize the rhythm of life and take it all in stride.

THE MAGIC OF TO-DO LISTS

Knowing *what* to do is only part of the job. The second part is *doing* it. Here are a couple of tips to help you put into practice the things you learn to help you achieve greater success.

One of your best self-management tools is to make To-Do lists. These should be made every night before you go to bed. You will have all night to sleep on them. And in the morning, you will have your day mapped out.

Remember, when you know where you are going, you can take shortcuts. Or at the very least, you can stay on the right path and not be distracted by unproductive activities.

A SIMPLE IDEA THAT HELPED BUILD A FORTUNE

Back when Bethlehem Steel was a small, up-and-coming company, a young management consultant named Ivy Lee paid a visit. He spoke with Charles Schwab. Later Schwab's success was to make him the first man in history to earn a salary of $1 million a year. Obviously Andrew Carnegie, founder of the company, liked Schwab's ability to accomplish things.

Ivy Lee proposed that he help Schwab to find better ways to do the things necessary for the company's success.

Schwab told Lee that they already knew how to make steel; they knew what needed to be done. But, he added, they were not getting those things done. Show me how to do the things we ought to be doing, Schwab challenged, and we'll pay you whatever you want.

Lee said he could do that in twenty minutes. He even offered to let Schwab use the system, and then pay Lee whatever the steel company executive thought it was worth, if anything. Schwab was impressed with Lee's confidence, and told him to proceed.

Lee handed Schwab a piece of paper and said, "Write down the things you have to do tomorrow." Schwab did as instructed. "Now number these items in the order of their importance," Lee continued. Schwab did that.

Then Lee gave Schwab his instructions:

"The first thing tomorrow morning, start working on Number 1 and stay with it until it is completed. Next, take Number 2, and don't go any further until that is completed. Then, proceed to Number 3, and so on.

"If you can't complete everything on the schedule, don't worry. At least you will have taken care of the most important things before getting distracted by items of lesser consequence."

Lee said that if Schwab completed every item on the list before the day was done, to make a new list and start on that. And any items that are left at the end of the day could be considered for the next day's list.

"The secret," Lee continued, "is to do this daily—evaluate the relative importance of the things you have to get done, establish priorities, record your plan of action, and stick to it."

Lee advised Schwab to do this every day, and to have others in the organization also use this system.

"Test it for as long as you like," Lee said, "and then send me a check for whatever you think the idea is worth."

In a few weeks, Charles Schwab sent Ivy Lee a check for $25,000, and that was back when $25,000 was real money. It was reported that Schwab told associates that this was the single most valuable idea he had ever received.

SOME SUCCESSFUL STRATEGIES

Neva Davis of Dallas, Texas, earned a lot of success in the industrial scales business, a tough business you wouldn't expect to find a woman running. She's an effective manager and dynamic salesperson. She has always been a big believer in setting goals, formulating plans, and keeping lists.

"During the Silva Method training," she said, "I wrote down all the techniques so I could check off how I had used them; the dates and times I used them.

"One of the first things I started doing was writing down my programming in a stenographer's pad, writing the date and even the time of day I had programmed each project. I began to fill that notebook up with projects. It was sort of like keeping a diary, but instead of keeping a diary of what was happening, I was keeping a diary of my programming.

"Now, when those things happened—and they did—I would go back to that page where I had written it down and write things like 'Success!' I got different colored pens so it would catch my eye. I'd write 'It happened!' 'It works!'

"Can you imagine when you get a whole stenographer's pad of successes filled up and you can look at it?" she asked. "When I would sit down to program another project, I'd pick up my stenographer's pad and look at it; I was tuning back to success, what it felt like to program that successful feeling.

"I reviewed the feeling of how it felt to program a project, and that it was successful, so I would adjust to that same state of mind again and be just as successful."

Art Thomas of Michigan also said that getting organized helped him improve his job and increase his income.

"My instructor Lou Barbone proved to be a patient, dedicated teacher who provided the combination to 'unlock the treasures' that were in my mind," Thomas said. "Soon after taking the course I became more organized and my energy level reached extraordinary heights.

"My business income rose dramatically," he continued. "By 1986 I had become a full-time investment broker with A. G. Edwards & Sons and was still maintaining my insurance business."

Thomas concluded that "The Silva course makes your 'strong points' stronger and can turn any weakness into a strength. It helps to unlock your mind and set it free to seek out the knowledge it needs to grow and perform efficiently for you."

It is important to be persistent, José Silva points out. He enjoys telling a story about a man who found a vein of gold. In his excitement, he lost the exact location, so he purchased the necessary equipment to help him locate the vein again. He searched and searched without success. Finally in despair, he gave up and sold the equipment to a dealer. The dealer decided to test the equipment before moving it . . . and located the vein. The dealer got rich, the riches that the first man could have had if he had persisted just a little longer.

INVEST YOUR TIME WISELY

Jim Ockley, Silva Method lecturer in Calgary, Alberta, Canada, tells a story about a couple of young boys, in their parents' absence, decided to take the grandfather clock apart, to see what made it tick, so to speak.

They took it apart and through some minor miracle seemed to get it back together. It wasn't quite right though, for sometime in the night it struck 123 times.

This startled their father. He sat up in bed, and shook his wife. "Myrtle, Myrtle, wake up! Danged if it ain't later than I ever thought it could be!"

For a lot of salespeople, it is later than they ever thought it could be. Each day of your life you are given 1,440 minutes, to do with whatever you wish.

Salespeople who spend those precious minutes in coffee shops, complaining about the economy, the sales manager, the lousy season their favorite ball team is having—those people are wasting one of their most valuable assets. They are throwing away something that they can never recover.

"To waste your time is to waste your life," Ockley says. "To master time is to master your life."

Get organized. Make a plan, and stick to your plan.

Eran Far, who sells insurance in New Jersey, says that business has been very good to her even though other people claim that there is a recession right now.

She has been programming to wake up at the proper and best time to review her agenda for the next day, and what she wants to accomplish. It is no surprise that her days have been going as she had planned.

Overall, Far said she has been doing less work with more effect.

MAKE A HABIT OF SUCCESS

Now that we have agreed on the importance of keeping records, to let us know where we are and where we are going, and of making To-Do lists, to get us moving and accomplishing things, let's consider how to make habits of these things.

A habit is a pattern of behavior that has been repeated over and over until it is easier to do it than not to.

There are bad habits, of course: overeating, drinking, and smoking in response to stress, for instance.

There are good habits also: brushing your teeth every night, and washing your hands after you go to the bathroom.

We tend to do all of these things without thinking about them. They are habits.

How can you make a habit of the actions and attitudes that will make you a more successful salesperson?

ANATOMY OF A HABIT

Your brain was programmed biologically, even before you were born, with certain survival programs. One of those programs causes you to become alert in the face of anything unknown. Instinct.

This stems from the days when our ancestors roamed the jungle looking for food. Other creatures were also looking for food. If your ancestor heard a rustling in the brush, he or she would get a quick burst of energy—adrenaline would pump into the bloodstream and boost blood sugar levels, he'd breathe faster to get oxygen into the system, his heart would race to pump the blood to tensed muscles.

All of this would enable your ancestor to run and catch the small animal and use it as a food source, or run away from the large animal and thereby avoid being used as a food source.

That programming became highly developed, because those who were best at it survived to have offspring, and the offspring inherited those characteristics.

You have inherited those enhanced characteristics.

The result is that anytime you encounter anything new in your environment, whenever you do not feel completely in control, anytime you are faced with change, your "fight or flight mechanism" kicks in and lets you know you've got to be ready for action . . . and for potential danger.

To put it another way, change represents a threat. In the jungle, they had to treat every unknown as a potential threat.

So, to avoid the feeling of being threatened, you can avoid change.

But if you want to become more successful, you've got to change. You have to start doing things that will help you become more successful.

You can see where the "fear of success" comes from. When you become more successful, that's a change. You often have more responsibility. You certainly have more money to spend or invest. Believe it or not, some people worry so much about whether they will spend their additional income wisely that they subconsciously sabotage their efforts to earn more money so they will not be confronted with this new responsibility.

GET USED TO SUCCESS, IT IS IN YOUR FUTURE

You may feel a bit apprehensive when you start practicing any techniques to help you become more successful. That just shows that you have a good fight or flight mechanism. As long as the techniques are new, as long as they represent something you are not accustomed to, you might notice this slight apprehension.

That's all right. Simply accept that as part of the growth process. It is a sign that you are doing it correctly.

Overcoming that feeling is very simple:

Keep practicing.

Make up your mind to keep on practicing the new behavior until you become accustomed to it. Once you are used to it, it will seem more natural to do it than not.

In other words, you will have developed a habit—a "success habit."

If you have developed the habit of brushing your teeth every night, and then one night you get in late and get in bed without brushing your teeth, you will probably feel uncomfortable as a result, perhaps so much so that you will get up and brush your teeth and then go back to bed.

The same thing happens when you get into the habit of entering your level every morning, of doing your To-Do list every night. Skip one of these activities and you will feel uncomfortable. That is, after you have done it enough to make it a habit.

How long does it take to create a good habit like this? Not long at all. In fact, ten days should be plenty of time. That is one reason we ask you to practice a technique for ten days—to make a habit of it.

Remember, you only use force in the physical dimension. When using mental techniques, the strategy is not confrontation, but cooperation. Relax, and use your greatest asset: your mind. Reflect on what you want, especially at level. Keep your thoughts positive, by thinking only about what you want. This will attract exactly what you desire. In the mental dimension, you do not use effort. You do use imagination.

IMITATE A SUPERSTAR

Navigating the road to success is easy when you have a map. You can follow in the footsteps of those who have gone before you, and then go on beyond.

Create your own success habits by finding someone you consider very successful and imitate their habits. They have already blazed a trail to success. Follow their trail, then use your own talents and energies to go beyond it.

Who is a salesperson you consider very successful?

Study this person. What do they do that helps them be successful?

Be careful when you make this study. In public, most successful people want to give the impression that they have plenty of time for you, that they do not have a whole list of things on their To-Do list.

But study these people carefully. Imitate what they do, not what they say they do.

You might find them getting up earlier and working later than the losers. You will find that they are well organized.

Notice also the "people skills" they possess, and let this guide you to making your own habits.

You can't be another person. You are unique, you are yourself. But when you see habits that are common to successful people, then it makes sense for you to create similar habits in your own life.

SUCCESS FROM THE INSIDE OUT

You can change habits more quickly when you work from within.

Willie is the one who runs the automatic operations in your life, so the quicker you can get the message to Willie, the quicker you will establish new habits.

Simply forcing yourself to do it over and over again will eventually get the message to Willie. But that's too much work.

There is a quicker way.

When you enter your level, you have direct access to Willie. You can program Willie for success.

To do so, simply enter your level and imagine yourself performing the activity you desire to do.

For the next ten days, as you practice your 25-to-1 count-down every morning, you can also imagine yourself practicing your new habit.

What new habit?

Imagine yourself at night completing your To-Do list, and during the day keeping records of each call you make. At your level, imagine yourself doing what you desire to do.

Then later, it will be easy to do it. In fact, it will be easier to do it than not to.

LOOK FOR THE GOOD, AND PRAISE IT

One final thought before we finish this chapter: Recognize feedback for what it is. If your task is getting easier, you are going in the right direction.

Remember Christopher Columbus? He was sailing west, searching for fame and fortune. His goal was a continent with untold riches. He sailed on faith, and somehow managed to keep his crew under control.

But his first sighting was not of a continent. First he saw some branches, some twigs, floating in the water.

Did he think that he had failed when his goal was a continent but all he found were twigs?

Far from it. He viewed the twigs as a sign of progress. If tree branches were floating in the water, could land be far away? The discovery empowered him, gave him renewed faith and energy.

Remember when you are working on your projects, as long as you are making progress, you are moving in the correct direction. Keep going. Never give up. You cannot fail . . . unless you quit. If you are not getting positive feedback, then adjust your direction. But always keep going.

We remember Christopher Columbus because he kept going until he reached his goal. Set your goals, make your plans, then keep going.

Assignments:

Your assignments for the next ten days are:

Start keeping records of every contact you make in your business;

Make To-Do lists every night and use them;

Practice entering your level by counting from 25 to 1 every morning, and imagine yourself developing new habits.

Record Book

This could be the *most important page* in this chapter. All superstar salespeople know the importance of keeping good records. You are a winner, and you will demonstrate it to yourself by recording your progress on this page.

Besides the countdowns, what is the most valuable technique you learned in Chapter 4? _____

How will this technique help you? _____

Why is this important to you? _____

Date used and results: _____

Practice Log:

Day 1   (25–1 countdown)   [ ]
Day 2   (25–1 countdown)   [ ]
Day 3   (25–1 countdown)   [ ]
Day 4   (25–1 countdown)   [ ]
Day 5   (25–1 countdown)   [ ]
Day 6   (25–1 countdown)   [ ]
Day 7   (25–1 countdown)   [ ]
Day 8   (25–1 countdown)   [ ]
Day 9   (25–1 countdown)   [ ]
Day 10   (25–1 countdown)   [ ]

Congratulations, you are now ready to go on to the 10–1 countdowns. Please turn to the last page of Chapter 5 and record your practice sessions there.

5

RELAX, IT'S GOOD FOR YOU

A young man admiring the view from atop a tall cliff stepped too close to the edge, slipped, and fell over.

As he fell, he thrashed about and somehow managed to grasp a small shrub. He could not find a toehold, and saw that the roots of the shrub were pulling out of the cliffside. Fearing that he had only a few moments before falling 1,000 feet to his death, he looked up for help. Seeing no one, he cried out, "Is there anybody up there who can help me?"

A voice from the heavens answered. "Yes. I am your guardian angel, I can help you. What do you need?"

"Get me back up on top," the young man pleaded as the roots slipped some more.

"Okay," the angel said. "I will get beneath you, then you turn loose, and I will catch you and place you back on top."

Let go? he thought. After a few moments silence the young man asked, "Is there anybody else up there who can help me?"

STRESS LIMITS YOUR OPTIONS

Salespeople encounter a lot of stress: appointments to keep, quotas to meet, objections to handle, the disappointment of lost sales.

Stress is part of life. In fact, we actually need some stress. Without a certain amount of stress in a couple of dozen muscle groups, you could not even stand up. Scientists refer to that as "positive stress." Negative stress is another matter. When stress becomes distress, it limits your options and can keep you in a bad situation even though there is something better if you could just relax and go for it.

Medical researchers readily agree that excess stress in your body can lead to diseases such as hypertension, high blood pressure, heart disease, respiratory diseases, ulcers and other digestive disorders, diabetes, stroke, heart attacks, and some researchers even believe that stress leads to diseases such as cancer.

Relaxing at the alpha level for fifteen minutes every day is healthy for you. It helps you to:

- Naturally counteract the stress syndrome;
- Strengthen your immune mechanism;
- Slow the aging process;
- Accelerate the healing process.

Stress can be caused by concern about survival, by worry over your ability to provide adequately for yourself and your family. It can come from fear—fear of failure, fear of success. Also, the need for approval can cause a great deal of stress.

And this stress, no matter what the source, can keep you from concentrating on what is most important: Customer Satisfaction.

You must move beyond fear and learn how to manage

the stress that you encounter so that you can better do your main job of serving and satisfying your customers. It is difficult to let go and accept help from a higher source when you are too concerned with the basic problems of survival.

CONQUERS FEAR OF PUBLIC SPEAKING

Furman DeMaris of Cherry Hill, New Jersey, used the Silva Method techniques that you will be learning in this and later chapters to overcome one of the most universal fears: fear of public speaking.

He first learned the Silva Method techniques in 1973, and a year later put them to the test. "I became a trainer for the state of New Jersey," he said. "I had to stand in front of an audience and teach. This was the greatest fear.

"I continued doing this through 1977," he said. "In September 1977 I joined Toastmasters to master the art of speaking. I became president in 1979, the area governor in 1982, and am now running for divisional governor.

"The Silva Method has given me the confidence I lacked as a child. I no longer have the fear of speaking in front of audiences. It has given me the confidence that has propelled me into Toastmasters and my job. I have been able to deal with people on a one-to-one basis, rather than in a subordinate position. It has also helped me to relax where I was tense and had severe headaches before."

STRESS SIGNALS: DO YOU KNOW WHAT THEY ARE?

How do you know when you are under stress?

Different people notice different things when stress strikes. For some, it is a tightness in the stomach. Others feel it in their muscles, as they knot up. Some get tension and migraine headaches.

Stress can affect your digestion, your concentration, your ability to make decisions.

One of the signs that you are under excessive stress—distress—is a failure to get along with people as well as you should. Do you get into confrontations instead of finding solutions? Look for stress as the culprit.

Stress manifests in many ways: It can hurt your health, ruin your relationships, clobber your ability to concentrate, spoil your memory and ability to recall information, and more.

Bette Taylor of Austin, Texas, saw her health suffer as she struggled to make a career in sales. Eventually she wound up bedridden with Ménière's syndrome, and doctors predicted she would remain in bed with the disease for the rest of her life.

Then she read a book about the Silva Method and began practicing the techniques. Later she took the Silva Method Basic Lecture Series.

Today, not only is Mrs. Taylor healthy and full of energy, but she has used the Silva Method techniques so successfully in her career that she serves as a consultant to numerous corporations.

STRESS IN YOUR LIFE: WHERE DOES IT COME FROM?

What causes stress in your life? Many people, when they are asked that question, think of money—or the lack of it. Deadlines can cause stress. So can having too many projects that need to be done immediately. Men sometimes say their wife increases the stress in their life. Wives counter that husbands cause stress. Both agree that raising children can be stressful. Of course the children say that their parents' demands and restrictions cause them stress.

There are many other stressors in our lives: The driver who cuts you off in traffic can trigger stress and cause you to start shouting about his level of intelligence and his probable ancestry, even though your car windows are shut and nobody can hear you except you yourself.

Paulette Temple of Oklahoma City, Oklahoma, could easily identify the causes of stress in her life: She worked for a major hospital as a dismissal clerk. Her job was to collect money due from patients as they were discharged. "Nobody likes to be asked for money when they are sick or hurting so you have some idea what I was up against," she said.

She went to level every day and used the Silva Method stress management techniques to control her own energy, and then used other Silva Method techniques that you will learn shortly. As a result, she says, "The majority of the patients responded with kindness and cooperation."

RESEARCHERS SAY SILVA DOES THE "IMPOSSIBLE"

Scientists identify two different kinds of anxiety:

- Things that happen—that threaten us, anger us, worry us—that can cause a stress reaction. This is called *state anxiety*.
- Personality traits and characteristics that cause a person to have a high potential to react with state anxiety when faced with a situation that the person perceives as menacing. This is called *trait anxiety*.

You have heard it said many times that we cannot always control what happens, but we can control our reaction to it.

The problem is, people develop habits through the years; they develop ways of reacting to situations. Willie learns these strategies, and no amount of rationalization by Wilfred is going to change it.

In addition, some personality types are just more prone to worry than others.

Until now, the "experts" have said that the only way to change these "traits" is through long, drawn-out treatment. You certainly could not expect a forty-hour program, presented over two weekends, to do it, the "experts" claimed.

But it happens.

In a research study conducted in 1984 under the direction of Dr. Moshe Almagor of the Department of Psychology of Haifa University in Israel, trait anxiety was "significantly lower" at the end of the forty-hour Silva Method Basic Lecture Series as compared to levels before the program.

Silva Method graduates were not only able to *act* more relaxed (manage *state* anxiety), but actually *were* more relaxed (decreased *trait* anxiety) according to the research.

What is so impressive about this research study is not just that people were less anxious and more relaxed after the Silva Method training, but that they continued to become even more relaxed after the training.

The average level of trait anxiety six months later was "significantly lower" again. As you might expect, there was greater improvement for those who practiced regularly than for those who did not.

"These facts illustrate the importance of daily practice in reducing the level of trait anxiety," the report notes, "although the trait anxiety level of those who did not practice daily, also improved considerably."

According to the researchers, the results of the study "contradict Spielberger's theory, which asserts that relatively short methods will not reduce the level of trait anxiety, but only the level of state anxiety."

THE SECRET OF THE SILVA METHOD'S SUCCESS

It is the ability of the individual to gain direct access to Willie and give new instructions that makes the Silva Method work.

"The specific feature of the Silva Method is to teach the subject to think in a state of relaxation, and while he is in this state, to utilize proper programming technique to accomplish fixed goals," the research report observes.

"The Silva Method is not hypnosis, because the subject is conscious and is completely in control of himself while practicing the techniques; he remains mentally active during the exercise, depending on no external agent.

"As opposed to biofeedback, [the Silva Method] provides techniques for the solution of specific problems, and it requires no apparatus."

In those statements, the researchers summed up the "secret" of the Silva Method's success.

Anything applied from the outside only treats symptoms.

When you do it yourself, you treat the cause.

That is why the Silva Method has worked better than hypnosis, yoga, biofeedback, and other procedures. The Silva Method succeeds where they succeed, and also succeeds where they fail—*because you are helping yourself.*

"The course provides efficient means for reduction of the level of trait anxiety," the research report concludes. "There are indications that, in spite of the influence of modifying variables, the method exerts significant influence on trait anxiety."

STRATEGIES TO RELIEVE STRESS

What do you do to relieve stress, to dissipate the energies that build up when stress strikes?

Many people take the "use it and lose it" approach. They use physical activity to get rid of all the energy that is stored in their body as the result of stress. They exercise, or participate in some kind of sports activity, or go dancing.

Others report that music is good for helping them unwind. For some, a hot bath is the perfect way to release the tension that causes the muscles to knot up and ache.

A lot of people say that hobbies help them unwind and

relax. One man said that gardening works for him. "If someone has given me a hard time," he explained, "then I think about them when I am weeding the garden. When I grab a weed, I imagine grabbing that person, and pulling them up and throwing them away. So if you ever have the feeling of being uprooted . . . " he smiled. . . .

A lot of people resort to three of the things that are vital to our survival: food, liquids, and air. You cannot live more than a few weeks without food, a few days without liquids, or a few minutes without air.

Do you eat when you are under stress? This is one way that many people reassure Willie that they are all right, that even though they are under stress, they won't starve.

Many people drink to escape the stress. Besides reassuring the body that there is no danger of dying of thirst, some liquids can also provide an escape mechanism. Besides drinking alcohol, some people take drugs for the same purpose.

Smoking has always been associated with relieving stress. One noted psychologist even observed that it gives people an opportunity to see their breath. And feel it, too.

ACTION RELIEVES STRESS

Here is a story about how one man reportedly dealt with stress:

He was a long-distance truck driver. Once he got his eighteen-wheeler on the road, he would travel for several hours. Then when he stopped, he wanted to relax and enjoy a good meal and good company.

On one trip, he stopped at a favorite diner, and asked his favorite waitress for his favorite meal: thick steak, baked potato with all the trimmings, chef salad with the special house dressing, and the homemade hot apple pie with a big scoop of ice cream melting over it.

Just as she was bringing the meal out, four grubby, mean-looking motorcycle punks swaggered into the diner.

They spotted the truck driver and went over and sat down on each side of him.

One took his steak, picked it up, and began gnawing at it.

Another took the big salad, poured the whole pitcher of dressing over it, and started shoveling it into his dirty mouth.

The third took the potato, smashed it up with the sour cream and cheese and bacon bits, and started cramming it into his mouth.

The fourth dug into the homemade hot apple pie, the ice cream running down his scraggly beard.

The truck driver sat for a moment, looking at their taunting expressions, then got up without saying a word, went to the cash register, paid his bill and left.

"Boy, he sure wasn't much of a man, was he?" one motorcycle rider sneered at the waitress.

"No," she answered with a shake of her head and a glint in her eye. "And he wasn't much of a truck driver either. He just ran over four motorcycles as he was driving out of the parking lot!"

INSTANT STRESS REDUCERS

Here are two more strategies you can use to short-circuit stress and cut it off any time it strikes.

First, take a deep breath, and relax as you exhale. Part of the flight or fight response is rapid breathing, to get more air into the lungs and oxygen to the muscles. When the emergency is over, we take a big "sigh of relief." So, let it out—the air in your lungs, that is. It will help you to relax.

Because of our flight or fight programming, most people use the worry technique instead of the solution technique. You can change that. After you have surveyed the situation, stop worrying about it. When people are too tense, they do not think as clearly. This leads to arguments and confrontations and poor decisions. Change your thoughts. Daydream about some peaceful place you know, as you did in your first alpha exercise in Chapter 1. This is the way to relax your mind. After you are relaxed both physically and mentally, then it will be easier to solve the problem you are facing. You can practice daydreaming about this peaceful place—your ideal place of relaxation—after you complete your countdowns.

Here is another strategy to help you instantly reduce stress: You can do what basketball coach Hector Chacon did in his story in Chapter 2—recall previous successes. When you encounter rejection, take a deep breath and relax, and recall a time when the prospect was willing to listen, and received a benefit as a result.

You can use a similar strategy when someone else is tense, and their tension and stress is affecting you. When somebody is uptight, tense, hostile, and their stress is making you tense also, then find a way to call their attention to something that they like and enjoy. Find something to compliment them on. Ask them a question about something you know that they are proud of.

This strategy was used by a customs inspector at the International Bridge between Laredo, Texas, and Nuevo Laredo, Mexico. During a Silva Method seminar, he asked how he could remain relaxed when the people he stopped became angry. People often became upset because they did not understand why they had been singled out to park their cars, get out, get their luggage out, and let him inspect it before they could come back into the United States.

"What technique can I use to relax myself?" he asked.

"Why not try this," the Silva Method lecturer suggested: "How about seeing what you can do to help them become more relaxed."

"How can I do that?" he asked. "They are being inconvenienced by me. They've just come back from a vacation, and now they have to stop and let us search them."

"You could look around and see if there is anything that they might be proud of, or want to talk about," the lecturer replied. "Maybe there is something special about their car, a special paint job, or custom upholstery. Or maybe you could say something nice about their children. Or ask them about the nice souvenirs they are bringing back, if they bargained and got a good deal on them, if they are a gift for someone special.''

He agreed to try this approach. A month later he came back and said it worked wonderfully. The best part, he said, was that he now experienced much less stress on the job, and frequently really enjoyed his job now because he was meeting such nice people and getting to know a little bit about them.

STRESS FOR SUCCESS: USE POSITIVE STRESS TO REACH YOUR GOAL

You can make up your mind to use stress constructively to help you reach your goal. The first step is awareness.

Stress is caused by anything that we perceive as a threat. And, thanks to our ancestors' early survival programming, we automatically consider anything unknown as a threat.

When you make a cold call, you are facing the unknown. It is natural to experience some apprehension. Of course, with enough experience, you will finally learn that a cold call does not directly threaten your survival—although it is certainly associated with your ability to earn a living and provide for your family.

If there were a way that you could use that energy to help you make a better presentation, make a better impression on your prospect, you would probably like to know more about that, wouldn't you?

José Silva has two techniques that you can put to use immediately to help you control stress and use it to help you make more sales.

We recommend that you practice this relaxation exercise once a week. Then use the Three Fingers Technique as you need it.

Here's José Silva to explain what to do.

PROGRESSIVE RELAXATION

You have already practiced counting backwards for thirty days. Now for the next ten days, shorten your ritual and count backwards from just 10 to 1. By the time you have completed the forty days, you should be reaching the alpha brain wave level by the time you get to the count of 1. The alpha brain wave level has been defined as being between seven and fourteen pulsations (or cycles) per second.

To help insure that you are reaching this level, you can practice the following additional exercise to accelerate the relaxation process.

Before beginning your countdown, go through a "progressive relaxation." This is the process of being aware of different muscle groups in your body, concentrating on them, and relaxing them specifically. It is usually done starting at the top of the head and going all the way down to your feet.

As you hold the book before you, eyes open, reading the instructions, actually perform "progressive relaxation." Then, tomorrow morning you will be able to do it without the book.

First, be aware of your scalp. Turn your attention to your scalp. Feel it. Know it is there. Feeling it may come in the form of a tingling sensation, or a feeling of warmth caused by the blood circulating in your scalp. If you relax your scalp, it will circulate even better. Relax your scalp.

Next do the same with your forehead. Be aware of your forehead. Let your imagination help you feel the tingling sensation, the feeling of warmth caused by circulation. Relax your forehead.

Relax your eyes, and the tissues surrounding your eyes. Feel the tingling sensation, the feeling of warmth, and then relax your eyes and the tissues surrounding your eyes.

Now concentrate your sense of awareness on your throat, the skin that covers your throat. Sense the tingling sensa-

tion, the feeling of warmth caused by circulation, and then relax your throat.

Continue relaxing your body one part at a time. Be aware of your shoulders, your chest, your abdomen. Notice your clothing in contact with each part of your body, and the tingling sensation and feeling of warmth. Then relax that part of your body and move to the next part.

Continue in the same manner to become aware of the rest of your body, part by part, relaxing each in turn: your thighs, knees, calves. Also your feet: your toes, the soles of your feet, and the heels of your feet.

Even though you are still reading, still mentally active, you should be able to feel the physical relaxation that you have just induced. You will know what to do tomorrow morning in order to enjoy this same deep physical relaxation. You will use progressive relaxation just before you begin your countdown.

And remember that after the ten days are completed, to continue to practice this progressive relaxation at least once a week. It will help you maintain your ideal level of mind.

THREE FINGERS TECHNIQUE

While at your level, you can pre-program yourself to be more relaxed in stressful situations. You will use a technique called the Three Fingers Technique.

In the Silva Method Basic Lecture Series, we use the Three Fingers Technique for stronger self-programming, and to help produce a better memory. Now I will show you how to use it to help you stay calm and manage your energies in stressful situations.

Enter your level as you have been taught to do. Once at your level, you can program yourself.

The first step is to bring together the tips of the thumb and first two fingers of either hand, or both hands. Bring them together in a circular shape. A lot of energy radiates *out of your body through your fingertips. This technique recirculates some of that energy so that you can use it for stronger self-programming. At the same time, this technique serves as a physical trigger mechanism: Every time you bring the tips of the thumb and first two fingers together, whatever you programmed for will happen.*

So while at level, and after bringing together the thumb and first two fingers of either hand, or both hands, tell yourself mentally that, "Anytime I am tense and desire to relax, all I need to do is to bring together the tips of the thumb and first two fingers of either hand, or both hands, as I am doing now, take a deep breath, and as I exhale, I will relax physically and mentally. And this is so."

Reinforce this at level from time to time. Then, when you need to relax, all you need to do is to bring together the tips of the thumb and first two fingers, take a deep breath, and relax as you exhale.

Record Book

This could be the *most important page* in this chapter. All superstar salespeople know the importance of keeping good records. You are a winner, and you will demonstrate it to yourself by recording your progress on this page.

Besides the countdowns, what is the most valuable technique you learned in Chapter 5? _____

How will this technique help you? _____

Why is this important to you? _____

Date used and results: _____

Practice Log:

              Day 1   (10–1 countdown)   [ ]
              Day 2   (10–1 countdown)   [ ]
              Day 3   (10–1 countdown)   [ ]
              Day 4   (10–1 countdown)   [ ]
              Day 5   (10–1 countdown)   [ ]
              Day 6   (10–1 countdown)   [ ]
              Day 7   (10–1 countdown)   [ ]
              Day 8   (10–1 countdown)   [ ]
              Day 9   (10–1 countdown)   [ ]
              Day 10   (10–1 countdown)   [ ]

Congratulations, you are now ready to go on to the Silva Method formula-type techniques presented in the next chapter.

6

STRESS-MANAGEMENT
TECHNIQUES

6

SELF-MANAGEMENT TECHNIQUES

The little girl said to her daddy, "Mamma sure doesn't know much about little girls."

"What do you mean?" he asked.

"Well, she tells me to go to bed when I'm not sleepy, and makes me get up when I am!"

SELF-PROGRAMMING TECHNIQUES

Congratulations. You have completed the forty days of practice with the countdown exercises and the fractional relaxation, and now all you need to do to enter your level is to relax, close your eyes, and mentally count backwards from 5 to 1 and you will be at your level.

Now that you have learned to go within, and to communicate directly with Willie while at your level, you can program to correct a wide variety of problems, and you have new strategies available to you, to help you achieve your goals.

Let's turn the podium over to José Silva right now to teach you techniques to overcome four problems that plague many people, and are especially harmful to salespeople: insomnia, oversleeping, tiredness, and headaches. If you need these techniques, use them. If you don't need them, they still serve as excellent models of how to program to overcome problems.

RESEARCH HELPS US UNDERSTAND SLEEP

There is no need for you to ever have a restless night, after you have learned the Sleep Control Technique. You may need to use it regularly, or you may need it only occasionally; either way, this is an important technique to learn. It can help you when you travel to different time zones, for instance, giving you the ability to sleep anytime, anywhere, without the use of drugs. With the irregular schedules that salespeople often have, this can be a very valuable technique. We often need to meet clients early in the morning before they get tied up with work, and sometimes we are on the road late at night working to meet our quotas.

When people use drugs to help them get to sleep, these drugs tend to interfere with the normal sleep and dream cycles. When you sleep at night, your brain cycles through all different frequencies, from the alpha frequencies of light sleep and dreaming, through the deep theta frequencies and all the way to the very slow delta frequencies of deepest sleep.

Sleep deprivation studies have shown that it is important that you spend sufficient time at the alpha level during sleep. When you are deprived of alpha sleep, there are serious side effects, such as irritability, loss of ability to learn and to recall information, and sometimes even mild hallucinations.

If you use drugs to induce sleep, they will interfere with the brain's normal rhythm and probably rob you of valuable alpha sleep time. Then you might need a stimulant in the morning to get going.

Obviously, none of this is good for a salesperson.

WHY PEOPLE DON'T SLEEP

Generally, when a person is unable to get to sleep at night, or has a very restless night's sleep and wakes up tired in the morning, it is because he or she is dwelling on problems.

Worrying about problems can make it difficult to get to sleep at night.

It can also make you reluctant to get up in the morning.

In the Sleep Control Technique, we give you something to do so that you will not be thinking about your problems. But the task that I will assign to you is boring, so boring that you will soon go to sleep.

There are three important points to remember about applying this—and any other—mental technique:

1. *The technique must be applied from the alpha level, not from beta.*
2. *You need to pre-program the technique to work for you.*
3. *You must be determined to make the technique work, and expect it to work.*

USING INSTANT SLEEP CONTROL

When you are ready to go to sleep, and you desire to use the Sleep Control Technique, enter your level and apply the Sleep Control Technique.

First, visualize a chalkboard. By visualize, I mean to recall a chalkboard that you have seen before. Then imagine that you are standing at the chalkboard with chalk in one hand and an eraser in the other.

Then imagine drawing a large circle on the chalkboard. Then mentally draw a big X within the circle. You will then proceed to erase the X from within the circle, starting at the center and erasing toward the inner edges of the circle, being careful not to erase the circle in the least.

Once you erase the X from within the circle, to the right and outside of the circle, write the word "Deeper." Every time you write the word "deeper," you will enter a deeper, healthier level of mind, in the direction of normal, natural, healthy sleep.

Then write a big number 100 within the circle. Proceed to erase the number 100, being careful not to erase the circle in the least. Then to the right and outside of the circle, go over the word "Deeper."

Then write a big number 99 in the circle; erase it; and go over the word "Deeper." Then continue in the same manner with the numbers 98, 97, 96 and so on until you fall asleep.

PRE-PROGRAM THE TECHNIQUE TO WORK FOR YOU

Most people know at least a little bit about personal computers. You know that in order to use the computer, you need to first install a program into the computer. That is, you turn on the computer and install a set of instructions.

Then when you want to use the computer, you turn it on, call up the program that has been installed, and use it.

Programming your brain is similar.

First we need to install the program. This is done by pre-programming yourself at the alpha level. Then when you need to use the program, you enter your level and use it.

Here is how to pre-program the Sleep Control Technique:

1. Enter your level with the 5 to 1 method.
2. Tell yourself mentally that anytime you need to go to sleep, you will be able to do so with the use of the

Sleep Control Technique.

3. *Visualize a chalkboard, and mentally go through the process described above, going back to the number 96.*

4. *Remind yourself mentally that anytime you need to go to sleep, you will be able to do so with the use of the Sleep Control Technique.*

5. *Count yourself out of your level.*

TAKE CHARGE OF YOUR LIFE

Remember that it is important to want *the technique to work, and to expect it to work.*

If you are just trying it out and are willing to give up easily, it may not work for you. Willie knows whether you are serious or not. If Wilfred is a big skeptic, Willie will get the message and you will not go to sleep.

But if you make up your mind that you are going to keep using the technique until you fall asleep, then you will fall asleep. Willie will get the message.

They say that there are three kinds of people in the world: people who make things happen, people who watch things happen, and people who wonder what happened.

If you just sit back and wait for something to happen, you will often find yourself wondering why things are not happening for you.

It is better to make things happen.

TO AWAKE CONTROL

In the To Awake Control Technique, we have an automatic system for using your mind to assist you in achieving goals.

At the alpha level, you can give instructions to your mind to cause an effect in your body. You instruct your mind to awaken your body at a specific time.

Here is how you apply this technique:

At night, when you are in bed ready to go to sleep, enter your level with the 5 to 1 method. Once you are at your level, visualize (recall) a clock. Mentally reset the time on the clock to indicate the time that you want to awaken, and tell yourself mentally, "This is the time I want to awaken, and this is the time I am going to awaken."

Remain at your level, and go to sleep from level.

You will awaken at your desired time, feeling fine and in perfect health.

Remember that you must first pre-program this technique. Enter level and tell yourself mentally that you can use the To Awake Control Technique to awaken whenever you desire, without a clock. Then mentally review the technique and imagine using it. Finally, before coming out of level, remind yourself that you can use the To Awake Control Technique to awaken whenever you desire, without a clock.

HOW YOUR MIND INFLUENCES YOUR BODY

Who keeps time? Your mind, which is not physical and therefore never needs to sleep, keeps time for you.

How does your mind wake you up? Sometimes you might awaken thinking that a barking dog, or a car horn, awakened you. This is the way your mind uses imagination to get your attention. Or you might awaken without realizing why.

We are not concerned with how you get up in the morning. Our real goal is for you to develop your ability to use your mind, to build a foundation that will be valuable to you later as you learn additional techniques.

By practicing this technique, you will develop your "Mind Control" ability, and will function better with techniques that you will learn later, especially techniques that involve mind-to-mind communication.

One of the first things you learn in the Silva Method is

how to use your imagination to relax your physical body. Now you are going a step further and learning how to use imagination as a communications tool to work consciously with your mind in the mental dimension to cause an effect in the physical dimension.

HOW TO BE MORE ALERT INSTANTLY

The Awake Control Technique is designed for use anytime you are drowsy or sleepy or feel low on energy. This could happen if you are driving home after a late-night appointment for instance.

As with all other Silva Method techniques, this mental technique is to be applied at level, after you have pre-programmed it as described earlier.

There are five steps involved, and these five steps are found in one form or another in the other Silva Method techniques. Each step is important; if you leave one out, there is a good chance the technique will not work as planned.

Here are the five steps:

1. Recognize the existing situation.
2. Establish your goal.
3. Make a plan for reaching your goal.
4. Apply the method that you planned.
5. Take it for granted that you have succeeded.

AWAKE CONTROL TECHNIQUE

Here is how to use Awake Control for learning to remain awake longer:

Whenever you feel drowsy and sleepy, and don't want to feel drowsy and sleepy, especially when you are driving, pull to the side of the road, stop your motor, and enter level with the 5 to 1 method.

At level, mentally tell yourself, "I am drowsy and sleepy; I don't want to be drowsy and sleepy; I want to be wide awake, feeling fine and in perfect health."

Then tell yourself mentally, "I am going to count from 1 to 5. At the count of 5, I will open my eyes, be wide awake, feeling fine and in perfect health. I will not be drowsy and sleepy; I will be wide awake."

Count mentally, slowly: 1, 2, 3; at the count of 3 mentally remind yourself that, at the count of 5, "I will open my eyes, be wide awake, feeling fine and in perfect health."

Then mentally count slowly to 4, then 5; at the count of 5 and with your eyes open, tell yourself mentally, "I am wide awake, feeling fine and in perfect health, feeling better than before."

Remember, it is important to take it for granted that you will feel refreshed.

It is much like using an assumptive close when selling. After you have shown the prospect how your product will benefit him or her, and the prospect agrees, then you assume that they are going to buy. Do the same when using the mental techniques of the Silva Method. After you have applied the formula, assume it has worked. Act as if it has worked. Pretend it has worked. Even if it doesn't feel as if it has worked, pretend that it does feel as if it has worked. Tell yourself a little fib and pretend that you feel refreshed and alert, and you will feel refreshed and alert.

Make up your mind that you are going to make it happen and Willie will get the message.

HEADACHE CONTROL TECHNIQUE

Doctors advise us that most headaches, possibly 90 percent, are caused by tension. Few are organic in nature. Whether you "have" a headache because of organic reasons, or "feel" a tension headache caused by stress, you can learn to relieve the pain with the Headache Control Technique.

If your headaches are caused by excessive stress, then you will obtain permanent relief by applying the technique; the headaches will occur less and less frequently until your body forgets how to cause them.

But if the headaches continue to recur with the same regularity, then you can suspect an organic cause, and should definitely seek medical attention immediately.

The Headache Control Technique uses the same five steps as the other Silva Method techniques: First, state the problem; Second, state the goal; Third, make your plan to reach the goal; Fourth, implement the plan to reach your goal; Fifth, take it for granted that it worked. Make up your mind and make it happen.

Remember, you must apply this technique at your level, after you have pre-programmed it. It works best when you apply it at the first sign of a headache.

Here is the formula:

If you have a tension type headache, enter level with the 5 to 1 method. Once at level, mentally tell yourself, "I have a headache; I feel a headache; I don't want to have a headache; I don't want to feel a headache.

"I am going to count from 1 to 5 and at the count of 5, I will open my eyes, be wide awake, feeling fine and in perfect health. I will then have no headache. I will then feel no headache."

You will then count slowly from 1 to 2, then to 3, and at the count of 3 you will remind yourself mentally that, "At the count of 5, I will open my eyes, be wide awake, feeling fine and in perfect health; I will then have no discomfort in my head; I will then feel no discomfort in my head."

Notice that we have made a change at level 3, from ache to discomfort. We left the ache behind. You will then proceed to mentally count slowly to 4, then to 5, and at the count of 5, and with your eyes open, you will say to yourself mentally, "I am wide awake, feeling fine and in perfect health. I have no discomfort in my head. I feel no discomfort in my head."

If you have a migraine headache, apply the same for-

mula, but use three applications, five minutes apart.

The first application will take care of part of the problem. The second application will take care of more of it. With the third application, the headache will be gone.

From then on when symptoms appear, one application will take care of the migraine problem. As you continue to take care of this problem in this manner, the symptoms will appear less frequently, until the body forgets how to cause them, bringing to an end the migraine problem with the use of drugs.

To correct health problems, controls are applied under a doctor's supervision. Consult your doctor and work under medical supervision.

CORRECTING THE CAUSE OF THE PROBLEM

You might be wondering why I say that when you use this technique as I have instructed you, this will bring the problem to an end and you will stop getting headaches.

It looks as though we are only treating the symptoms, and not the cause of the problem.

With almost any other technique, that would be true. A hypnotist can program you while you are hypnotized and get rid of your headache, but he will not correct the cause of the problem. As a result, you will continue to get headaches. Aspirin will correct the symptoms, but not the tension that is causing the headaches.

However, when you enter your level yourself, on your own, and you apply the formula yourself, then what you are doing is telling Willie that you want him to correct the cause of the problem.

Then Willie will do whatever is necessary to correct the cause of the problem. You may not ever be aware of what was done to correct the cause of the problem, but Willie knows.

SHE REDUCES STRESS AND WINS NEW JOB

You can use the same approach—the same five-step formula—to deal with other problems that you may be facing.

Here is how Paulette Temple used the Three Fingers Technique, which you learned in Chapter 5:

She was doing such a good job as a patient account manager at the hospital where she worked that she was offered a job as account manager at a prominent corporation with five psychiatrists, a psychologist, and two psychiatric social workers. "They offered me a salary the hospital could never match," she said, "and asked if I would come for an interview with the president of the corporation.

"If you have never been interviewed by a psychiatrist, you have never been interviewed!" she continued. "I had only five days to prepare for the interview." She entered her level twice a day and programmed a successful interview, as you will learn to do in Chapter 8. And she reinforced her programming with the Three Fingers Technique.

"After shaking hands with the doctor I sat down and put together my three fingers, expecting the conditioned response I had programmed for all week to take effect: relaxation, in tune with the doctor, and answering all his questions honestly and with just the right amount of enthusiasm.

"The interview lasted an hour and when I left I felt I had gotten the position. Three days later this was confirmed."

PROGRAMMING OVERCOMES LIFELONG FEAR OF FLYING

Have you ever seen someone with a fear of flying? It can paralyze them, make them physically ill.

Allen Rose, a columnist with a Central Florida daily

newspaper, had been plagued with fear of flying for more than thirty years. Then he learned the Silva Method.

"I had tried everything," he recalled. "I had read every book on the subject I could find. Even called a guy halfway across the country who taught a course for white-knucklers. I knew *all* of the statistics about airplanes being the safest way to go. Nothing worked. I had to almost soak myself in alcohol to go near a plane."

Even though Wilfred knew that flying was safer than riding in a car, Willie was still plagued with that irrational fear.

But after Rose knew how to enter his level and give new instructions to Willie, he eliminated that fear.

"Since the Silva course," he wrote in his column, "I have taken four flights. Couldn't wait to get aboard the last one. Now, I wouldn't hesitate to jump on a jet tomorrow for anyplace in the world. And that, friend, is a circumstance I had long ago considered impossible in this life."

PROGRAMMING TO BANISH FEAR

His Silva instructor, Betty Perry, explained that Rose used "a very simple technique to overcome his fear of flying.

"I suggested something I had read about in the Silva Method Newsletter," she said. "José Silva said if you have a fear, admit to the fear and it will never happen again." Rose used the five-step formula outlined, with the outstanding success you just read about.

"I've told many people to use this technique for fears, and they've been very successful," Perry said.

Do you ever get nervous when you are around other people, or have to talk with them? Consider the story of a lady who had agoraphobia when she came to the Silva Method.

"She would get anxiety attacks in public places," Perry said. "The first weekend of the class, she stayed in her room to eat. Then she used the technique to get over her fear.

"The second weekend, she ate in a restaurant for the first time in four years."

The story gets better. "When I called to see if she was going to repeat the next class," Perry said, "she said, 'I can't.' I asked what she meant. She told me she was taking a trip to Panama. When I asked who was going with her, she indignantly said, 'By myself!'"

OVERCOME DEBILITATING STROKE

Betty Perry herself is a great success story. Here is how Allen Rose explained it in his column:

"Betty Perry is one of those delightful people who always appears upbeat, positive, purposeful," he wrote. "It's a pleasure to be around this vibrant, healthy, smiling lady. I get a lift every time I talk with her.

"But it wasn't always this way," Rose continued. "A stroke in 1966 left her with partial paralysis, a speech impairment, and an outlook that she describes as 'terrible.' She wore corrective shoes and had to lock her knee to go up steps.

"'My memory was lousy, I had vision problems and I was depressed,' she said. 'I ate all the time.' Her weight ballooned to 175. She was frustrated that life had dealt her such a blow in the prime of life.

"'Doctors kept me alive and got me to the point where I was able to get around,' she said. But they told her there was nothing more they could do. They said she had brain damage and was lucky to be alive. All of that went on for fourteen years.

"Today, it would take a neurosurgeon to detect a trace of the problems that once beset Betty, a former operating room nurse and former wife of a St. Petersburg orthopedic surgeon. Her words are clear now. She has lost forty pounds. Her memory amazes her friends. At a recent convention party, she danced for hours.

"She attributes her recovery to the visualization and

mental techniques she learned in 1980 through the Silva Method,'' Rose concludes.

How did Betty program to overcome the stroke?

She made up her mind to do it.

She went to level three times a day, usually for fifteen minutes each time, and applied Silva Method techniques similar to those that you are learning in this book. They are taught in the Silva Method Basic Lecture Series, and you can read about them in *You the Healer*, written by José Silva and Dr. Robert B. Stone (H. J. Kramer).

Record Book

This could be the *most important page* in this chapter. All superstar salespeople know the importance of keeping good records. You are a winner, and you will demonstrate it to yourself by recording your progress on this page.

What is the most valuable technique you learned in Chapter 6? _____

How will this technique help you? _____

Why is this important to you? _____

Date used and results: _____

SUCCESSES

Date	Technique Used	Results
_____	_____	_____
_____	_____	_____
_____	_____	_____
_____	_____	_____
_____	_____	_____
_____	_____	_____
_____	_____	_____
_____	_____	_____
_____	_____	_____

7

CREATIVE DREAMING

A story is told that in ancient times there was a city named Gordia that had no ruler. The citizens of Gordia felt that they were so evolved that they did not need anyone to rule them.

Allowing for the possibility that there might be someone wise enough to rule them, they devised a test:

At the gates of the city was tied a chariot. Anyone who could demonstrate his or her wisdom and ability by untying the knot, loosing the chariot, and riding it through the city could rule the people.

But all who tried—and there were many—failed to untie the Gordian Knot. It was so big and so tangled that those who tried could not even find an end of the rope so that they could begin to untie it and loose the chariot.

Then one day there rode to the gate a young man who called himself Alexander the Great. Not overly concerned with modesty, his goal was to rule the entire world.

"You mean to tell me," Alexander said, "that all I have to do is loose the knot, free the chariot, and ride it down main street and you will submit yourselves to my rule without a fight?"

The citizens of Gordia confirmed this. With that trial close completed, Alexander the Great simply drew his sword and with a swift stroke cut through the Gordian Knot, rode the chariot through town, and claimed his reward as ruler of Gordia.

HOW TO DEVELOP WISDOM

Now comes the part of the book you have been waiting for. You have paid your dues by practicing the countdowns for forty days, and you have already reaped some rewards in the form of several self-management techniques.

Now you are ready to take a gigantic step forward and learn several techniques to help you shape your life and your career the way you desire.

The ability to see things from different perspectives, and to correct more problems than the average person, is the beginning of what people refer to as wisdom.

AWAKEN THE GENIUS THAT'S SLEEPING WITHIN YOU

People who do all of their thinking with only the left brain hemisphere are far more limited than those who use both brain hemispheres to think with.

We see a perfect example of that in the story of the Gordian Knot.

Until Alexander the Great came along, everyone approached the problem logically.

But Wilfred—whose domain is logic and reason—could not solve the problem.

It took someone who could see things from a different perspective—from Willie's perspective—to solve the problem by going straight to the end result.

Of course some people will say that Alexander cheated—he was supposed to untie the knot. That is one of Wilfred's characteristics, to rationalize and come up with some kind of an answer, even if it is untrue or has nothing to do with the situation.

Willie will come up with illogical, unconventional, new, innovative, creative, practical solutions for any problem you ever face.

This is wisdom. At least, it is part of wisdom. Another part of it is being able to convey information effectively to others, and to implement the solutions you come up with. We will cover that later.

There are several ways to get information from Willie:

- You can enter your level and think about the problem while at your level. Be sure to maintain minimum mental activity; if you find yourself becoming aroused or upset, you are probably listening to Wilfred again and you probably are no longer at your level.
- You can use your imagination to create imaginary helpers that you can imagine discussing things with while at your level.
- One of the best, most natural, easiest, and most reliable ways to get information and ideas from Willie is through dreams.

UNDERSTANDING YOUR DREAMS

Scientists tell us that everybody dreams, though not everyone remembers their dreams.

What are dreams? Researchers are not entirely certain, but it seems that dreams are necessary for us, in order to file away information that we have received during the day.

Dreams take place at the top of Alpha. You recall that when people are deprived of alpha sleep, they suffer a number of detrimental effects: fatigue, irritability, loss of memory, inability to concentrate, and even hallucinations. This is why we gave you a technique to go to sleep without drugs—so you can get plenty of alpha time during sleep.

When Wilfred goes to sleep, then Willie can go to work

without interruptions or interference from Wilfred.

But if Wilfred does not like the messages that Willie sends through dreams, then the person might stop remembering the dreams.

But the dreams are still there, and you can learn to recall them. And even more importantly, you can learn to interpret and understand them.

And best of all, you can learn to control your dreams. You can put Willie to work at night to find a solution to a problem.

You say there are too few hours in the day to do everything that you need to do? You say you have a prospect who needs your product and you can't understand why he won't buy it?

Then call on Willie to do the job at night while your body sleeps.

Willie will give you new insight into the problems you are facing. And Willie will also bring you help from the other side, from the spiritual dimension.

HOW TO INTERPRET YOUR DREAMS

What do your dreams mean? You can learn to interpret your own dreams and use them to help you make more sales through practice and through the study of the most interesting person in the world: you.

We each have our own unique experiences in this life, and so each of us adopts unique patterns of symbolic expression of the events in our lives. You can learn about the symbolic expressions you have programmed into your "bio-computer" by using the Dream Control Technique that José Silva will teach you in just a moment, and then keeping a dream log, or dream diary, of all the dreams you have.

When you awaken with a dream, write down a brief account of what the dream is about. In the morning, enter your level, and write out a more detailed account of the dream. Be sure to write it down as soon as you have it. Transfer it to the physical dimension, or you risk losing the memory of it.

In the morning, review the dream stories you have written down. Then enter your level and ask yourself about each dream, "How could this dream relate to what has been happening in my life?" This will help you to understand the symbolism you use, and over a period of time, you will gain so much understanding that you will interpret very rapidly.

This can be one of the most effective exercises you will ever do to assist you in understanding yourself better, and your purpose in this world. Make up your mind to work with your dreams.

YOU CAN LEARN TO CONTROL YOUR DREAMS

Now for the ultimate step: controlling your dreams, and using them to solve problems.

There are many benefits to controlling your dreams:

- You will eliminate unpleasant dreams, and dream only of what you desire.
- Willie will explore your memory banks and inner conscious levels and give you creative answers to problems based on your past experiences.
- Willie and Will can scan other people's brains for information to help you make decisions and solve problems.
- You will develop greater control over the alpha dimension, and you will develop more skill in creating and controlling images within this dimension.

Here are some ways that programmed dreams can help you:

AVOIDING BAD DEALS

Charles N. is a contractor in Albuquerque, New Mexico. He was very skeptical about taking the course. "Give me a check at the start of the course," the lecturer told him. "We will be in class all day Saturday and Sunday. Wait until Sunday evening and then tell me whether you want me to deposit your check, or return it to you."

Charles agreed and started class on Saturday morning. Saturday night he decided to program a dream to give him guidance on a big (and expensive) project he was planning to undertake.

On Sunday, he had a story to tell the class:

"I dreamed about an old friend of mine, a boy that I grew up with," he related. "We even roomed together in college, and graduated together. Then we went into a business venture together.

"Eventually we went our separate ways," Charles continued, "and I had not thought about him in thirty years.

"Naturally, I began to wonder why I dreamed about him last night. I went to my level and thought about it, and do you know what I realized? I realized that the reason we have not seen each other in thirty years was because of the way we parted company after that business deal. It cost me a lot of money.

"The more I thought about it," he went on, "the more I realized that there were many similarities between that deal with my old friend, and this new deal I have been working on. I have decided that before we proceed any further, there are quite a few questions that I want answered."

During the night, Willie had scanned Charles' brain cells, going back through all of the old memories, to find information that could help him today, and perhaps save him a lot of money.

CREATE YOUR OWN IDEAS TO SOLVE PROBLEMS

Many people have had dreams that contain creative ideas for solving problems.

Carolyn Deal, Silva Method lecturer in Greensboro, North Carolina, has "dreamed up" many newspaper advertisements that have made her a lot of money. "Ironically, when the ads created professionally by expensive agencies brought no one to my classes," she said, "my dreams produced ads that brought hundreds of people."

One ad was headlined, "I hear the best stories in Greensboro." Several brief stories from satisfied Silva Method graduates were included in the ad.

Another ad shows a picture of Deal hanging on to an airplane that appears to be in flight. The headline reads, "The sky is not the limit." In this long ad, she tells her own personal story. She used to be a withdrawn, self-taught artist but now, thanks to the Silva Method techniques, she is a dynamic, outgoing individual who loves people. She has also been one of the top producers in the Silva Method for several years.

In 1977 Roman G. S. Barba, Sr., of Manila read José Silva's book, *The Silva Mind Control Method*, and started something he couldn't finish. He came up with two inventions that won him international recognition and major awards, but he couldn't find the right formula to make them feasible for the marketplace for more than ten years.

Then in 1988 Barba attended the Silva Method Basic Lecture Series with lecturers Yu Bon We and Judy Qua in Manila. Before he completed the second weekend, he had answers to his problems.

In his dreams he came up with answers that worked. He was so happy that he wrote the following to José Silva:

"Because of the tremendous help your Silva Method has

been to me as an inventor and a science researcher, I am pledging a portion of my future income from the above two inventions for the propagation of your Silva Mind Control Method in my country by sponsoring interested individuals to learn your Method.''

PENNIES FROM HEAVEN? HOW ABOUT DOLLARS FROM A DREAM!

"Results from the techniques presented in the Silva Method can be both quick and dramatic," according to Alan Phillips, a new-age musician and direct marketer from Lovingston, Virginia.

"When I first signed up for the Basic Lecture Series, I had only enough money for the first weekend of the two-weekend course. During the first weekend, one of the techniques taught was the Dream Control Technique, through which the instructor insisted that graduates could acquire problem-solving insight and information not readily available to their conscious mind and outer senses.

"And so having completed the first weekend and being faced with the prospect of not having the resources to finish the course, I began fervently 'programming my dreams' to get information on how I could get the money to complete the course.

"The instructor, Paul Fransella, had spent a great deal of time explaining how dreams usually provide us with information through symbols, and cited numerous testimonials in which that had been the case. The dream that resulted from my programming efforts, however, was quite literal.

"I dreamed that I asked my father for the money. In the dream, he sat down at a small desk and wrote out a check, as I stood by looking over his right shoulder.

"At that particular time in my waking life, my relationship with my father was such that even if I had consciously considered asking him for the money, I would have immediately dismissed the notion. But having had the dream, I thought, 'Oh, well, what have I got to lose?'

"I called him and presented him with my dilemma. It turned out that he had heard of the Silva Method from a friend of his (much to my surprise), and he was quite unexpectedly open to my request for support in finishing the course. He invited me to come by and pick up a check for a personal loan.

"When I arrived at his house, he invited me in, and sat down to write out a check. As he wrote out the check, I noticed that the physical surroundings and our respective locations were, as far as I could tell, identical to the dream! The room, the desk, the angle and location of my visual perspective—everything seemed a carbon copy . . . except for one thing: While this action was physically taking place, I was thinking to myself in a rather uniquely amused and amazed frame of mind, 'This is just like the dream.'

"I remain convinced to this day that even if I had purposely tried, I could not have forced the physical actions to occur in the manner they did, identical to the dream. José Silva has certainly devised a potentially powerful methodology!

"Obviously, as this and other even more dramatic examples of the Dream Control Technique demonstrate, dreams have the power to inform us about resources of which we are not consciously aware, and we have the potential to control our dreams to have them provide us feedback on our own personal needs and desires."

DREAM TELEPATHY

Was there some way that Willie knew that Alan Phillips' father would be willing to loan Alan the money for the course?

Research conducted at the sleep and dream laboratory of the Maimonides Medical Center in Brooklyn, New York, presents a strong scientific case for that very thing. In their book *Dream Telepathy*, published by Macmillan Publishing Co. in 1973, researchers Montague Ullman, M.D., and Stanley Krippner, Ph.D., report on many cases where mental telepathy seemed to take place while a subject dreamed.

While one research subject slept, another waited for the right time to project mentally to the sleeping subject. When the sleeper was awakened and asked about the content of his dream, he would frequently give a report that matched the thought that was being beamed his way.

José Silva put this into more practical terms in his research. He asked a mother to program herself to awaken at the ideal time to communicate mentally with her young son while he slept. The boy had been wetting the bed all of his life, and she wanted very much for him to stop.

They had planned to repeat the process for thirty days to see if they could get any results. But on the very first night, the boy, who was staying with a relative in another city 150 miles from Laredo, woke up in a dry bed.

The boy never wet the bed again after that night.

CAN WE HARM PEOPLE WITH THE MIND?

José Silva decided this might be a good time to find out once and for all if it is possible to create a problem mentally, at level, at a distance, so he asked several experienced psychics to try to program the youngster, at a distance, to start wetting the bed. The boy never wet the bed again.

This has led Mr. Silva to believe that there is no way that we can use these levels, at a distance, to cause a person to do something that is not in their best interest.

Willie can ask Will to deliver a message. But in this dimension, there is only cooperation, not confrontation. The other person has Free Will, and will do only what is in their best interest.

In the physical dimension, we can use force to hurt one another. In the spiritual dimension, we can only help one another.

As Mr. Silva puts it, we prey on each other at beta, but we pray for each other at alpha.

Is there a way that salespeople can use this to make more sales? There certainly is. We call it broadcasting, and we will explain it in Chapter 14.

DESTROYING MONSTERS

It is human nature to fear whatever is new. Remember our discussion of our cave man and cave woman ancestors in the jungle. When they heard the rustling in the bushes, they were immediately on guard, alert and ready for action.

The spiritual dimension is a new frontier for us to explore. The science of psychorientology is just beginning to map this new territory. We have been at it only since 1944!

Sometimes people encounter experiences that they do not understand, and the flight or fight response kicks in.

Psychorientology research is helping us to understand what is going on, so that we can stop fearing that "rustling in the bushes" and can use this dimension to help us correct more problems and reach more of our goals.

Here is a problem that José and Paula Silva ran into one night.

They were visiting Monterrey, Mexico, and left their children with a baby-sitter in the hotel while they went out for the evening.

The baby-sitter wanted to watch television, so she told the children to stay in bed or the bogeyman would get them. As she told them this, she tapped her hand against the wall and told the children, "Hear that? That's the monster, and he will get you if you get out of bed!"

The children stayed in bed.

This may have solved the baby-sitter's problem, but it created another problem for the children. Now they were afraid to get out of the bed after dark to go to the bathroom, or to get a drink of water.

It did no good for their father to assure them that there

was no such thing as a bogeyman. They knew better: At night, they could "see" the bogeyman . . . in their imagination. "But that's not real," their father tried to convince them. "It is your imagination." They were not convinced.

Then he hit on an idea to remedy the situation. "The next time you see the bogeyman," he told them, "you point your finger at him and shake your finger at him as hard as you can. Every time you shake your finger, that monster will get smaller and smaller and smaller," he said.

The youngsters started shaking their fingers rapidly, until they had shrunk the monsters down to a very small size, so small that they could hold the monsters in their hands.

After that, there was no more problem with bogeymen.

"People sometimes let their imagination get the best of them," Silva said. "They imagine things so vividly that they paralyze themselves; they are afraid to take action, because of the monsters they have created with their imagination.

"It is like a psychosomatic illness," he explained. "If you fear something enough, then you can bring about the very condition that you fear. It is like Job said in the Bible, 'That which I feared the most has come upon me.' But you are doing it to yourself, nobody else is. The good news is that you have the power to change it, simply by changing your mind. Make up your mind to change, and use the Silva Method techniques, and you will change."

You make the changes just as you learned in the last chapter: At your level, acknowledge the problem, state your goal, outline your plan, take action, and claim your end result. You can do this to eliminate nightmares, slay monsters, or change anything that you want to change.

In the next chapter, we will show you how to eliminate many of the monsters that salespeople face: fears such as the fear of making cold calls, fear of telephones, fear of asking for the order.

But first, here is José Silva to tell you how to develop your ability to use your dreams to solve problems.

DREAM CONTROL TECHNIQUE

It appears that we each have a minimum of four sleep and dream cycles each night, each cycle lasting about ninety minutes. This gives us ample opportunities to utilize dreams and thus benefit in many ways.

The earlier sleep and dream cycles are the deepest and have short dream periods. Later cycles are much lighter and have longer dream periods.

By programming yourself, you can awaken at the ideal time to recall your dreams. If you awaken too early, there is no dream, if you awaken in the middle of the dream, you may be confused, but when you awaken near the end of a dream, you can remember it and understand it. Since you will be at a very light level of sleep, it will be very easy to open your eyes, make a few notes about the dream, then close your eyes and go right into the next sleep and dream cycle.

So if you do not have enough time during the day to do all that you want to do, learn to use a portion of your sleep time to get more done.

Start by programming yourself to remember one dream. We call this Dream Control Step 1.

To practice remembering a dream, you will enter your level with the 5 to 1 method. Once at level, you will mentally tell yourself, "I want to remember a dream, and I am going to remember a dream." You will then go to sleep from your level.

You will awaken during the night or in the morning with a vivid recollection of a dream. Have paper and pencil ready to write it down. When you are satisfied that Dream Control Step 1 is responding, then start with Dream Control Step 2.

To practice remembering dreams, you will enter level with the 5 to 1 method and then mentally tell yourself, "I want to remember my dreams, and I am going to remember my dreams.'' You will then go to sleep from level.

You will awaken several times during the night and in the morning with vivid recollections of dreams. Have paper and pencil ready to write them down. When you are satisfied that Dream Control Step 2 is working, then start with Dream Control Step 3.

You can use Dream Control Step 3 to practice generating a dream that you can remember, understand, and use for problem solving. Enter level with the 5 to 1 method. Once at level, mentally tell yourself, ''I want to have a dream that will contain information to solve the problem I have in mind.'' State the problem and add, ''I will have such a dream, remember it, and understand it.'' You will then remain at your level and go to sleep from level.

You may awaken during the night with a vivid recollection of the desired dream, or you may awaken in the morning with a vivid recollection of such a dream. You will have this dream, remember it, and understand it.

Remember that it is best to pre-program yourself at your level, before using this technique. Enter your level with the 5 to 1 method and program Dream Control Step 1. When you are ready to use Dream Control Step 2, then enter your level and pre-program yourself to use Step 2. Do the same with Step 3 when you are ready to use it.

Record Book

This could be the *most important page* in this chapter. All superstar salespeople know the importance of keeping good records. You are a winner, and you will demonstrate it to yourself by recording your progress on this page.

What is the most valuable technique you learned in Chapter 7? _____

How will this technique help you? _____

Why is this important to you? _____

Date used and results: _____

SUCCESSES

Date	Technique Used	Results
_____	_____	_____
_____	_____	_____
_____	_____	_____
_____	_____	_____
_____	_____	_____
_____	_____	_____
_____	_____	_____
_____	_____	_____
_____	_____	_____
_____	_____	_____

8

CREATIVE VISUALIZATION

*One night I was awakened by a tapping on my window.
That seemed strange because my bedroom is upstairs. I got
up and looked out and saw that my brother was throwing
pebbles at my window to wake me up.*

*He told me that our sixty-two-year-old father had suf-
fered a heart attack and was in the hospital in critical condition.*

*I hurriedly dressed and rushed to the hospital. I per-
suaded them to let me go in to the room where my father
lay. There were tubes running into his body, wires con-
necting him to machines that were worriedly blinking and
flashing and beeping and humming. He looked terrible. He
seemed so small and helpless. I was scared.*

*I took his hand, gently. He did not move. Then I closed
my eyes, entered my level, and imagined him getting better,
growing stronger, being disconnected from all of those
tubes and wires, being moved into a private room, coming
home, resuming his work of managing our family business,
a welding shop. While doing this, I could hear the rapid
beeping of the monitoring equipment begin to slow down
and level out.*

*When I finished, I opened my eyes and looked at him
again, in that tangle of tubes, so small. . . . Then he opened
his eyes and looked at me. It might have been my imagi-*

nation but it seemed as though his eyes smiled at me. Then he closed his eyes again. I knew that everything would be all right, and I knew that he knew this too.

As I walked back to the waiting room, I looked to my left and saw people sitting there, worried, crying. I looked to my right and saw more people, upset, concerned, eyes red from crying. And I thought to myself, "Thank God I will never have to stand by helpless again when a loved one needs help."

My father recovered completely, and continued to manage the welding shop for another decade.

—DENNIS HIGGINS

There have been countless books written by successful authors extolling the manifold virtues of visualization.

You can use your mind to create the kind of world you want for yourself, they tell you. You can shape your life and everything in it to suit yourself, they say.

They insist that visualization is the key to reaching your goals, to achieving all that you want in life. They are living proof, because they have done it. So, too, have some of their students. Sometimes they even admit that 90 percent of those who follow their methods fail; but those who persist, they tell you, will succeed.

Does that number sound familiar: 90 percent fail, 10 percent succeed?

What these authors don't tell you, because they don't know, is that *the real key to success is the ability to function at the alpha level with conscious awareness.*

Get the idea? *You already know how to function at the alpha level.* At this point, you can take any of those books and start using their techniques successfully. You couldn't do that before, unless you were one of the 10 percent who had somehow learned, through natural means, to get to the alpha level. But now you can get the results you desire from the self-improvement books, because you can enter the alpha level and apply the techniques there, like the superstars do.

You can also continue to read this book and learn the

latest scientifically researched techniques to help you get the most from your visualization. These techniques are designed to help you obtain repeatable results.

In fact, when you learn to use the scientifically researched and proven techniques of the Silva Method, you will be even better off than those who developed their abilities on their own. Why? Because you will be able to coordinate your efforts with other people who use the same techniques, to get even better results. You can join with other Silva Method graduates in a sort of master mind alliance, all working together, in the same manner.

VISUALIZATION AND IMAGINATION DEFINED

First of all, let's define some terms.

You *see* with your eyes. Anytime you attempt to focus your eyes, your brain adjusts to twenty cycles per second beta frequency. In order to be at alpha, with eyes open or closed, you must be sure not to make any attempt to focus your eyes and see directly with your eyes.

You *visualize* with your mind. To *visualize* means to recall what something looks like, something that you have seen before, or something you have imagined before. Visualization is memory, the memory of what something looks like.

To *imagine* means to think about what something looks like that you have never experienced before, something you have not seen before or visualized before. It is a creative process, because what you are thinking about is something you have never seen or imagined before.

Visualization is not like seeing. It is not even like dreaming. It is like remembering. It is remembering what something looks like.

Here's an example:

Do you remember seeing, on television or in a movie, the dog Lassie? (If not, then recall any dog that you have seen.) Do you remember what the dog looked like? What size is this dog? How big? How long was the hair? What color was it? What did its tail look like? Its ears?

Remembering what you have seen before is visualization. And you have just visualized a dog that you have seen previously.

How many legs did that dog have? Four? Now, can you imagine what that dog would look like if it had six legs? Where would the other two legs be: At the front? The back? In the middle? Where would they be? Imagine what that would look like.

Now you have just used imagination to create a mental picture of something that you have never seen or imagined before. It is very simple. You can do it with your eyes open, or closed. You can do it at beta or at alpha.

In order to imagine things and have them manifest in the physical world, your visualization and imagination must be at alpha. For now, it is easiest for you to do this with your eyes closed, because you shut out distractions. Later, with practice, you can learn how to function at alpha with your eyes open and defocused. Creative daydreaming can be done at alpha.

Now, if you go back and recall that dog you imagined with six legs, and you recall what the dog looks like and where the two extra legs are—the front, the back, the middle—then you are visualizing, because you are recalling what something looks like that you imagined previously.

Now let's consider how you can use visualization and imagination to help you make more sales.

HOW VISUALIZATION TRANSFORMED MARGE LIDDY'S LIFE

Marge Liddy says that goal setting, positive thinking, and visualization helped her build a very successful real estate business, persuade the man she loved to marry her, and more.

Along the way she learned some valuable lessons.

"You have to be careful what it is that you decide you want," she said. "Once you become obsessed with an idea that you want something and you are going to make it happen, I can verify that you have to be careful, more than likely you will get it."

Her experiences emphasize how important it is that you use the subjective dimension, instead of putting all of our faith in your objective tools.

Liddy graduated from the Silva Method Basic Lecture Series in May of 1973, and used the Method extensively. She hosted cottage group meetings of Silva graduates in her home, and even helped organize classes.

In 1974 she purchased a very small real estate business in Satellite Beach, Florida. "It was owned by a husband and wife, and they had four listings," she recalled.

Within two years she had built her new business into one of the biggest real estate companies on the beaches of south Brevard County, and the fourth-largest and most successful in the area. They had three separate offices and some sixty sales associates.

She taught her sales staff how to use visualization and imagination to make more sales.

"I used to do a walk-through with the staff in my sales office," Liddy said. After having them close their eyes and relax, "I'd have them imagine putting sold signs in front of their listings.

"But you had to take it a step further," she added. "Not just imagining a sold sign, but take them to the closing table, their hands on the table, and getting their check. A sold sign in front of the house doesn't necessarily mean it will be sold.

"I would encourage my people to keep a positive outlook, and to use positive thoughts," she continued. "I encouraged them to go take the Silva Method Basic Lecture Series, but most of them were struggling so they didn't have the cash to do it. You know how that goes: You need the doctor, but can't afford to pay for it."

She also programmed hard for her personal goals, especially in regards to a man she had started dating in 1972. She made up her mind to marry him, and eventually did.

"I was so much in love with this guy that I didn't know which end was up," Liddy said. "Once I learned the process, I started visualizing the wedding. It did take two years for it to materialize. We got married in 1975." He was also a realtor, and they were partners in the real estate business.

"The marriage was not something he wanted as much as I wanted," she admitted, "so therefore I forced something to happen that was not in his best interest.

"Sometimes you can get so involved with these things that you only decide what is going to make you happy, not what is going to make everybody happy. You can forget that you have to program for the best thing for all concerned. That's a real good point, that needs to be brought out: for the good of the whole."

In 1981 they were divorced, and she sold two offices and gave her remaining interest in the business as part of the settlement.

Liddy acknowledged that if she had programmed to find out what was best, and followed the guidance, she would have been better off.

Instead, she used every technique she could think of to develop her powers of persuasion and to find arguments in favor of marriage, and finally convinced him to marry her.

"I can tell you that I made it happen," she said. "I did have some reservations about doing this. Some little voice down deep said that this wasn't fair." So she persuaded him to attend the Silva Method training for his own self-defense.

"He used it quite a bit. He visualized things he wanted to happen in his life. He visualized a boat at his boat dock, and sure enough, one appeared. So it definitely does work."

After the divorce, Liddy wanted out of the real estate business. She felt that the business was at least partly responsible for the breakup of her marriage.

"I was really kind of burned out, because when you go as hard and fast as I do, it is easy to get burned out."

She invested her money in a ceramic tile business, with

her son as a partner. "The competition was terrible," she said, "and quickly absorbed all my money.

"Everybody kept asking me why I didn't go back into real estate, because that's what I know best. Because I don't like it, that's why! I fought it tooth and nail."

Then she learned two valuable lessons.

A friend came to Liddy one day and told her that her dream house had come on the market. This was a riverfront house in Palm Bay, Florida, that Liddy had admired for a long time. But it was tied up in an estate; they could not get a clear title because of a missing heir.

"I got the MLS book, looked it up, and it was offered for an unbelievable $89,000," she said. Boy, it needed a lot of work! However once remodeled, it was appraised at $175,000. I knew it was really what we realtors call a Handyman Special and I could turn a good profit. I had no money. The ceramic tile business was taking all of my time, energy, and money, trying to make a go of it. I was out there working it. I said there was no way I could buy the house."

Her friend told her, "I have an idea that if you want it bad enough, you will figure out a way."

"I guess I had a kind of waking dream and it kind of weighed on my mind, so the next day I decided I had to give it a shot. One way or another, I had to figure out a way to buy it."

She wrote out a contract on the property with a $100 deposit. "I took it to the listing realtor and there were two other contracts ahead of mine. I told them to put it in line and see what happens." There was no way she could have honored the contract at that time, because all of her money was in the ceramic tile business, but she had faith and imagined herself living there.

Two years later, both of the other contracts had fallen by the wayside because they still had not cleared the title. Liddy waited patiently. By now the ceramic tile business was turning a nice profit.

"Then I sold the ceramic tile business, along with the building that we had purchased, and I had a nice pot load of cash just about a month before the title became clear on this property. Now I had the only contract on the house." So she bought her dream house!

"Even though the ceramic tile business had been a very difficult business, I sold it at a profit mostly because of the building," Liddy explained. "Real estate has always saved me. It has been good to me. I've had my periods when I hated it with a passion, but it has always made me a good living."

She had learned that she could accomplish whatever she wanted when she really wanted to, and that her expertise was in real estate.

After that, she did two important things:

"I went back and took the Silva course again, and started thinking positive, getting my mind in the right direction, which was: What you put your attention on is what you accomplish the most with. If you scatter your attention, you scatter your energy. It taught me to go to level, and to pinpoint my energies again, to put them in the right perspective."

After reviewing the Basic Lecture Series with Betty Perry, Liddy began to use the Silva Method techniques to get guidance on what to do with her life. She also enrolled in the graduate course.

The result?

"Now I am working as an independent real estate broker," she said. "It is working very well for me. My old clients find me somehow. They call me. I go and give them my undivided attention. If they have a house to sell, I take that particular house and work on it until I sell it. I do a lot of visualization around the house."

The combination of the two things—the Silva Method techniques, and the real estate business—allows her to live a very comfortable, happy life.

"I'm not wealthy, but I'm certainly living very comfortably for a lazy middle-aged lady," she laughed.

She has an active social life, including a man she has been dating for seven years.

Programming for guidance, and then focusing her energies to do what's best for all concerned, has helped Marge Liddy create a life filled with the happiness, prosperity, and sense of fulfillment that everyone seeks. Just always remember to program your needs to the good of the whole, Marge urges. She learned the hard way.

ANYONE CAN SELL WITH VISUALIZATION

Visualization and imagination at the alpha level are such powerful tools that they even help people who are not sales professionals sell when they have to. Joyce McCarty of Dalhart, Texas, sold her house after real estate agents failed to, even before she completed the Silva Course.

"I decided to sell my house around the first of August in 1979," McCarty wrote to Silva International, Inc. "I was visiting with my sister in Dallas when a real estate agent called me from Dalhart and asked if I was interested in selling the house. At the time, I did not have the house listed.

"I told the agent I would pay him a commission if he sold the house for $45,000. The real estate agent informed me that the savings and loan would only finance for eighty percent of $38,000. He also told me I should take the offer on my house and sell it, or forget it.

"I decided not to accept the offer.

"When I arrived home from my visit, I had a long-awaited card from Johanne Blodgett that she was having Silva Method classes on two consecutive weekends. I decided to attend these classes.

"On Saturday," she continued, "I put an ad in the paper to sell my house. The first day the ad ran was on the following Tuesday. On Friday of the same week, I left my store to drive to Lubbock for the first session. I might add that before I left, I took four aspirins for a headache and relief of tension (I have not taken any aspirin since).

"The first weekend of the Silva Method class, we were to use the Mirror of the Mind visualization technique on something we wanted accomplished immediately. Of course, mine was to sell the house.

"The next week I showed my house to three different people. Before I went back for the second session on the next weekend, I had sold the house for $45,000.

"The savings and loan officer handled all the transactions without charging me a fee. He also loaned ninety percent of the $45,000," she added.

"I know that any way you look at it, my $200 spent on the course was well worth the money. In a sense, that fee was returned to me by the sale of the house many times over.

"This one event was only the beginning of the rest of my life."

USING TECHNIQUES FROM SILVA BOOK MADE STEVE REDPATH AN EXTRA $7,662

Steve Redpath of University Heights, Ohio, used the visualization technique taught in the book *You the Healer* by José Silva and Dr. Robert B. Stone (H. J. Kramer) in his publishing business.

"Because of this one technique," he said, "I earned an additional $7,662 over the previous year."

Redpath said he used a 10 to 1 countdown to enter his level, then would spend approximately ten minutes visualizing his goals. "Then I would *immediately* get on the phone," he added. "Whenever I would use the technique, I could quickly focus on my customer's needs and how to serve them."

NETWORK MARKETING BUSINESSES BENEFIT FROM VISUALIZATION

Eleven sales representatives of the Mary Kay Corporation attended the Silva Method Basic Lecture Series and applied the techniques.

Within a matter of months, nine of those eleven had become directors.

"That high a percentage, achieving that progress in that time, had never happened before," according to Ginger Grancagnolo, the Silva Method lecturer who taught them the course. "These girls have now duplicated themselves, and are now a group of twenty-two directors."

"I heard Mary Kay on television talk about how she turned her life around, understanding the power of prayer and so forth," Grancagnolo said. "She is training character, she is not just pushing a product. I became very interested in this."

She is also one of the natural alpha thinkers, so when she prayed, she got results.

When the Mary Kay sales representatives learned to enter the alpha level and function with conscious awareness, then their prayers also worked.

The Mary Kay training program contains all positive thinking elements, Grancagnolo said. "As I would say things, the girls would say, 'We learned that in our training, about positive thinking, and success is a feeling from within that then creates action.'"

The Mary Kay program emphasizes three aspects of life: "These are, God first, family second, and career third," according to Grancagnolo. "In the Silva Method Basic Lecture Series we discuss particular ways the girls can use the various mental techniques to help them achieve their goals, and how to arrange their schedules so that they can take care of family and husband and children and business, to economize on their time.

"There are a few companies of this type that really need form for their substance," Grancagnolo continued. "What they are saying is all good stuff, but they still need direction."

PROGRAM TO OVERCOME DIFFICULTIES

Programming at the alpha level can help you to overcome difficulties that you may encounter.

Olga Malicki was a manager of a fashion store in a mall

in Massachusetts when she attended the Basic Lecture Series. She programmed to bolster her faltering business.

When she learned the programming techniques, she made up her mind to project for increased sales. She said she noticed an immediate change. Her store, which had never appeared on the company's "Big 10" sales list, made it soon after. The store's business had increased by 56 percent, and Malicki received a letter of congratulations from the company vice president.

Speaking from valuable experience, Malicki feels that it is really necessary to continue working on projections all the time in order to produce a steady flow of energy into a specific project. She has found that after that initial success, you want to become more and more successful, or to put it another way, "Better and Better."

Silva International Foreign Director Juan Silva, who assisted his brother José in much of the early research, says that the most valuable time to practice is "when you don't need to." Practice when things are good, Juan Silva urges, so that when you encounter a problem, it will be easy to enter your level and visualize a solution and feel that everything is all right.

"When you are relaxed and serene," he explained, "you will establish a firm baseline at an ideal level of mind. Then the techniques that you practice will be established much more positively, so that when you need them later, they will work very effectively for you."

Another graduate, M.S. of Sacramento, California, says, "I had begun my Monday telephone sales job by getting NO on every call. Very depressing. As I had just finished the first weekend of the Silva Method, I knew I should be able to do something to change all those NO's to YES. I went to the ladies room and did some heavy programming and sure enough, I didn't get another NO all day. Sensational!"

Now let's turn to José Silva for a visualization technique designed to help you make more sales and earn more money. This technique is similar to the Mirror of the Mind Technique taught in the Basic Lecture Series, but is easier for you to learn on your own.

JOSÉ SILVA TEACHES A VISUALIZATION TECHNIQUE

Let's create a tool to make visualization and imagination easier for you to use. We will call this tool the Mental Screen.

Your Mental Screen can be like a movie screen if you like. Imagine it out in front of you, a little higher than your horizontal plane of sight, about 20 degrees. You can imagine projecting mental pictures onto this screen.

If you prefer, you can imagine a television screen. Again, imagine it approximately 20 degrees above your horizontal plane of sight. Some people like a television screen because they can turn it on and off, and change channels when they desire.

Still other people prefer to use a computer screen. If you have used a Macintosh computer, for instance, then you know how easy it is to create pictures on the computer's screen. You can easily change them. And you can delete them with the touch of a button.

YOUR MENTAL SCREEN

You can use your Mental Screen to transfer anything you desire from the physical dimension to the mental dimension. Things are sometimes very difficult to alter in the physical dimension. For instance, a prospect may be clinging desperately to an old prejudice or a false belief, and not buying your product. It is difficult to get a person to change by arguing with them.

However, in the mental dimension, anything is possible. It is a very simple matter to make changes in the mental dimension. Here is how you would proceed:

First, enter your level and project onto your Mental Screen an image of the problem thing, person, or scene.

Make a good study of the problem. By that I mean to notice the details.

After making a good study of the problem, or the existing situation, then erase the problem image. Erase it, imagine it dissolving away, change channels, delete the image from your screen—do whatever you like to get rid of the problem image.

Then use your imagination to create the solution image you desire. In the example above, you can imagine yourself talking to the prospect, explaining things so that the prospect sees it in a new light and understands how you want to help him or her.

You have now converted your problem into a project. In the future, whenever you happen to think of this project, visualize (recall) the solution image that you have created.

Never again go back to the problem image. Anytime you think of the project, immediately recall the solution image.

You can reinforce this solution at level from time to time. Remember that you have already created the solution, and you are waiting for it to manifest in the physical dimension.

Remember, at the mental dimension, you use cooperation rather than confrontation to reach your goals. Relax and let it happen mentally, then go out and take the necessary physical steps to complete the project.

Now let's look at some more examples of how Silva Method graduates have used visualization at the alpha level to solve various kinds of problems.

HOW A TOUGH SITUATION YIELDS TO PROGRAMMING

Paulette Temple of Oklahoma City, Oklahoma, had a tough task: collecting the money after the service had been delivered. She had to collect bills from people who had been stricken with serious illness.

"As dismissal clerk at a local hospital," she said, "I dealt with patients when they were being discharged. I collected the difference between their total bill and what their insurance paid, plus a lot more.

"Nobody likes to be asked for money when they are sick or hurting," she said, "so you have some idea what I was up against.

"After going through the Silva Method Basic Lecture Series I began using my Mirror of the Mind technique and picturing every patient surrounded by love. Then I imagined myself asking the patient to give whatever it was I needed to complete his dismissal.

"The majority of the patients responded with kindness and cooperation," she continued. "As a result, my collections began increasing and I got a promotion.

"I carried all my techniques to a new job as I was promoted to a collector. The job as a collector was not only a pay raise but also a huge responsibility.

"I am now responsible for approximately $100,000 in my portion of the alphabet, A-F. This is an average of 725 accounts. My job consists of collecting money after all insurance and other benefits have paid and the patient has left the hospital. Most of my collecting is done over the phone and I have to be prepared to handle many different situations at all times.

"Each time I pick up the phone to call on an account I use my Mirror of the Mind technique. First I picture myself reviewing the file, understanding the problem or reason why I have this account, getting a good mental picture. I then picture the solution, whatever it may be to complete this patient's file and get his account paid in full.

"I keep this solution image in my mind all the time I am on the phone. It helps me to say the right words to the patient and make him want to pay his bill and feel good about it."

How well does this work? There are three other ladies in the department, Temple reported, all with many years' experience. "Since I became a collector seven months ago (with no previous experience) I have been the top collector in the office every month," she reported.

"Lately my co-workers have been asking me, 'How do

you do it?' I think at first they thought it might be beginner's luck. So I shared with them what I'm doing and they are becoming very interested in the Silva Method.

"My supervisor called me into her office the other day and expressed her happiness with the job I have been doing. She said I have created a competitiveness between the collectors and for me to keep the others chasing me.

"My goal is for the other collectors to become Silva Method graduates so we can all work more harmoniously together.

"Thanks to what I have learned in the Silva Method and applied in my daily life, I have been able to make the transition from a hairdresser to the top collector of a major hospital in a large city very effortlessly and very enjoyably.

"Thank you, José Silva, for helping me to awaken my genius within."

You can program yourself in the same manner. Whenever you feel rejected and depressed, take time out and go someplace where you will not be disturbed for a few minutes—like the rest room. Then use your Mental Screen and reprogram yourself. Erase the rejections, and imagine people accepting you and taking action—such as granting you an appointment or placing an order.

SALLY VANTRESS CHANGED HER WHOLE LIFE

Visualization and imagination can help you in your programming to overcome fear, guilt, and doubt.

When it comes to overcoming fears, Sally Vantress bit off a big chunk all at once. She made some really big changes in her life. Over the course of three years, she went from being a banker to an adventurer, riding her bicycle around the world, to author, lecturer, and very effective salesperson.

Every step of the way was fraught with fear. "Every fear I had, I faced on my trip," Vantress said. "I think every fear you ever have, you eventually face it; otherwise you don't move on with your life. Now I recognize when I am afraid of something, and say, Okay, this is not something to be afraid of. It is like, acknowledging it is ninety percent of the solution.''

As she neared the age of thirty, Vantress wanted a change. "I was a banker, a very skeptical, left-brained person," she said. "I knew that I wanted to travel, wanted a change. I did not want to travel the conventional way.

"Then I met Mark. He is the one who told me about Silva. He had just peddled across America on a bike. I had never seen that before. I had never seen a bicycle with bags all over it, I never knew that you could travel that way.''

She decided to go. "It was a real shock to my family. I had always been kind of adventuresome. I had learned to fly. They thought I had a death wish or something. I guess I like to put life on the edge. The family would never do that. My dad didn't know if I'd ever come back, but they didn't tell me that before I left. As much as they could, they were supportive; they never told me not to go. I don't know if they really understood why I was doing it. I didn't fully understand either.''

But go she did. After quitting her job and selling her house and airplane, she bought a bike and a book about the Silva Method and flew to New Zealand. "That Silva Method book was part of my mental preparation for the trip," she said.

"I had gotten a list of Silva Method lecturers from around the world. I thought, if one of these comes up, and I am in the country, I will attend.''

In New Zealand, she called Judith Sansweet and found that a class was coming up in about a week. That was perfect, and she attended.

It came in handy, because during the next nineteen months, Vantress peddled the bike 21,000 miles!

"All of this was new to me," she said of the Silva Method training. "I'm not sure I believed it all at first, but a lot of it I had to believe, because I was out there like a sitting duck.''

DAILY PROGRAMMING KEPT HER SAFE

"Every morning, before I'd start riding, I'd program to protect myself from getting into accidents. I never had an accident on my trip. That was something that was pretty strong with me. I was in situations where there was bad weather, on highways where trucks would blast by me within six inches, I had dark clothes, no bike lights; I had to believe that this was working and I wouldn't get hurt."

All of the people she met on her journey were kind and helpful, except for one ex-convict she encountered in Georgia, who gave her a hard time. "I think my fear attracted that situation to me," she said. Even though the situation was frightening, she came through it and continued her trip without any delay.

"I knew the trip would change my life," she said. "I thought I would get some specific questions answered, like, What do I want to be when I grow up? But I understood soon into the trip that I wasn't going to get those answers.

"Now it is real easy to look back and see that it served as a gap in my life, to kind of break up things and give me a chance to be out there and unwind, and start anew."

And things did happen. "Although I made it happen, I also believe that I was chosen to make it happen," she said. "As things continue to materialize, I have this feeling that I had guides that are pushing me along, to be an example for others. I've got a lot of trust that it is okay wherever it leads. I'm kind of like a river—I just go with the flow."

MENTAL PRACTICE PRODUCES RESULTS

The next step was writing. "People ask me, What do you do for work, Sally? Are you going back to banking? I tell them, Well, I wrote this book . . .

"I had no experience when I started my trip around the

world. I didn't even know how to change a tire. I had no experience in writing a book. When people told me I should write a book, should give talks, I thought they were crazy.''

She decided to do it, and visualization and imagination helped . . . a lot. The book, *Seeing Myself Seeing the World*, is available direct from Sally Vantress, Box 543, Capitola, CA 95010.

"I am very much a hands-on, visual person," she explained. "In the Silva program, when they first started mentioning the colors on the Mental Screen, they were right there for me.

"Whenever somebody explains something to me, immediately it is on my screen. I have always done that, since I was a child. When I learned to fly an airplane, I used to practice by visualizing. That's how I learned to fly instruments: Instead of reading the book, I'd sit in my room and imagine myself doing it. I did really well with instruments. It is not easy. The only way I think I made it through that was that I have a wonderful ability to visualize the things I have to learn.''

PROGRAMMING HELPS SELL MORE BOOKS

Now that her book is written, she uses visualization and imagination every day to sell the book.

"I visualize the books in the bookstore, and I light them up so that they are easy for people to see. I visualize at night, especially when I know somebody has bought a lot of books and they have a display, and I've seen it; I go to that store frequently in my visualization, and I make that display glow. I program that anybody who sees it will look at it, and that the right people who need that particular message that is in my book, will get the book.''

She expands on that to get speaking engagements. "The way I think of my book now, is that it is a lot of mini-brochures for me. I program that the right people will pick up that book and come into my life, to help through the next step.''

As she has continued to practice, she finds that programming is easier. "On my trip, there were certain times of day that I would meditate. Now it is just part of my daily life. I can do it anytime.

"The best is to lie quietly somewhere. Now, since my visualization is so good, I can do it while I am jogging. I think that I have incorporated it into my life and it is so subtle sometimes that I don't even realize I am doing it.

"As I am calling a bookstore, I visualize the promotion material that I've sent to them, and it will light up on their desk and they will know right where to find it when I speak to them.

"Another way is to scan my data base, look at it, and trust my intuition about who to call. Whatever notes I've put on there about when to call back are irrelevant when I listen to my inner voice.''

She feels that she projects thoughts that are received by other people. "I'm pretty sure I have a real loud broadcast. It is so interesting how you start thinking about people and they call you. And when I am out of town, I don't get phone calls. People seem to know when I am around, and they call me.''

PROGRAMS TO OVERCOME FEAR OF SUCCESS

Her fears showed up again and almost delayed publication of the book. "We had a book signing," she recalled, "but the printer ran into a problem and couldn't get the books out. I called the printer and told him we had to get it out. All of a sudden I was working out of fear and anxiety.

"I think I had a lot of inner fear: This book is ready to go to print, to be published; it is going to be on the streets. How is it going to be received? This is a book about me. If it is not received, have I been personally rejected?

"So subconsciously, there was a lot of anxiety there. As a result, the book got delayed. Then the truck was in an accident. Then the books arrived and twenty-five percent of them were defective. The strange thing was, some of the covers were slashed right through my face! Can you imagine seeing your face slashed?

"We had them ship four boxes of books by air to get there in time for a book signing. The night before, 10:30 P.M., they still had not arrived. I knew that my broadcast was so loud, that I had so much fear about seeing these books in reality, being a published author, that this was happening.

"So I sat there and visualized: I love these books, I want them, I am proud of them. I really had to work hard at trying to overcome whatever was in there that I wasn't facing, in terms of what my book was, and not trying to think about comparing it to other books, or what it ought to be or could have been. Boy, that was tough."

The books came, and they are selling well, thanks in part to her persistent programming. Her workshops are well received. And she is having the time of her life.

HOW TO CONQUER THE FEAR OF CALL RELUCTANCE FOREVER

Dave Bellizzi came down with a severe case of call reluctance shortly after he started selling insurance.

"I enjoyed my first day calling on people for appointments," he said. "I made about thirty calls and got three appointments. Applying the theory of ratios, I saw that I would get one appointment out of every ten calls I made.

"But after the second day, I hated making calls with a passion! I had called up this one lady and she yelled and screamed at me and cussed me up and down and sideways. I was what you would call shell-shocked. I never wanted to make another call again. Just the thought of picking up the phone would make my heart pound faster, my palms sweat, and my voice crack.

"After that experience," Bellizzi continued, "I went out of my way to find excuses not to call on people. I know every excuse there is because I used them all. Yeah, I'll call in a minute, I have something else to do right now. Business is bad. Business is slow. This is a very difficult product to sell. The price is too high. We need more advertising. Nobody's got the money now. Etc. Etc. Etc. Sound familiar?

"My sales manager was starting to catch on. He asked, 'What's the problem?' I answered, 'I don't have a problem.' He said, 'Let's find out. Let's go to your desk and I'll listen while you make some calls to see and hear what you're doing.'

"I panicked.

"I said, 'Okay, let me go to the bathroom first.' I started sweating buckets, and wondered what I was going to do.

"Then I got a brilliant idea. I went back to my desk and started dialing. I told my sales manager that the first one was busy. The second, no answer. The third one I made believe someone on the other end said that the person I asked for was not home. I was wasting time because I knew my manager had to leave in thirty minutes.

"Then on the next call I made believe I was talking to someone. My manager got excited. He kept saying, 'Good, now close for the appointment, close for the appointment.' I kept making excuses up and handling them perfectly, but making sure I didn't get the appointment.

"My manager got so excited he wanted to hear what was going on, so he picked up the extension. All he heard was . . . the box scores for the previous day's baseball game. I was calling the twenty-four-hour sports phone line, which was a pre-recorded message.

"That was the beginning of the end. He gave me all that talk about the law of averages, rejection, and so on, but it didn't help. I still couldn't make the calls.

"Even when I did somehow get an appointment with a prospect, I would do the same thing. I would get sick, have car trouble, sometimes I even got lost—on purpose, sub-consciously, I suppose. I used to pray that the prospect wasn't there. When I knocked on the door, if they didn't show after thirty seconds, I ran back to my car and left.

"It got to the point that I was filling out false records. I lied about the calls I made, the appointments I made, the presentations I made, the objections I got. But I couldn't lie about my sales. They were zero. That's when I decided to quit.

"Fortunately, I saw an ad that day for the Silva Method, and I took the course.

"It was after I took the Silva Method Basic Lecture Series that I realized what the problem was and how to over-come it. It was very simple.

PROGRAMMING: A QUICK CURE FOR CALL RELUCTANCE

"I programmed a dream the first night to find out what the problem was. I got a dream about that lady who chewed me out. Then I realized what was going on.

"Call reluctance is negative expectancy. I expected every-one I was going to call on to either reject me, yell at me, scream at me, give me a hard time, chew me out, say bad things about me or something else horrible. I really believed that. Why? Because on my mental screen, I was always visualizing that lady who gave me a hard time and I would always imagine everyone else doing the same thing. I wasn't aware of it, of course, until after I analyzed the dream. But with those mental pictures playing in my mind over and over, I believed that it would happen.

"So I decided to change the channel and watch another mental movie.

"You see, that kind of fear is nothing but negative ex-pectancy. We expect something negative to happen—neg-ative meaning, the opposite of what we desire. We play it on our mental screen, and watch it at some inner level. To us it is real, just as the bogeyman is real to a child. This negative image represents a threat and triggers the flight or fight mechanism and we become nervous and upset and we want to run from it.

"It is all happening at a 'subconscious' level, we are not even aware that it is happening. That is a big part of the genius of José Silva's discovery—that we are now able to convert the subconscious level to an inner conscious level. We bring the subconscious up to the conscious. With that awareness, we can understand the problem. And since we are able to function with conscious awareness at that level—the level that used to be subconscious—we can change whatever is there. All we have to do is give the right instructions to Willie while at level.

HOW TO REPROGRAM A NEGATIVE EXPECTANCY

"How do we do it?

"First, you've got to want to. You must have the desire to overcome your problem. Make up your mind to do it.

"Second, you've got to believe in what you are doing, and in your product. You are in the business of helping people, not bothering people, so you better believe in yourself and your product. If not, program it, or get into another line. When you know that you are helping people, then you do not feel as though you are bothering them or taking them away from what they are doing. They have a problem, and you have the answer that they need.

"Third, change your viewpoint or mental movie. You do that by entering level, acknowledging the problem, imagining the solution, making your plan, then implementing your plan with confidence that it will work.

"To overcome my call reluctance—call it fear—I imagined approaching either real people or make-believe people, and I imagined them thanking me for calling on them because they needed the help I was offering. I imagined them saying Yes to me because they desperately needed my help.

"I spent a lot of time at level programming like this to make sure that I had really internalized the idea that I was in business to help people. That is the reason that we are on this planet, according to José Silva.

"In fact, José Silva says that if we remember that, we will become very prosperous. He says that if you want to make a million dollars, and if you need to make a million dollars, it is very simple: Just give ten million dollars worth of service to humanity, and if you need to make a million dollars, you will.

"He says that the way he programs when he needs money is to program to give more service, and while programming he keeps in mind what his needs are . . . and a little bit more.

"Now you can do what I did. Every morning, before you start work, imagine yourself serving people and they are very happy to receive your service and pay for it.

"And remember, every time you call on someone, it is to help them. Selling is helping people, isn't it?"

FROM BANKRUPTCY TO PROSPERITY IN RECORD TIME

Brian Macdonald of Edmonton, Alberta, Canada, was already bankrupt when he somehow scraped up the money to attend the Silva Method Basic Lecture Series.

"I am forty-two years old, married with three children," Macdonald said. "I have been selling real estate in Edmonton, Canada, for nineteen years. In 1984 I first heard of the Silva Method by reading José Silva's book *The Silva Mind Control Method* [Simon & Schuster, 1977]. Real estate here had hit rock bottom after a three-and-a-half-year slide and a severe recession was just ending.

"I had practiced visualization on my own with moderately good results but it wasn't enough to save me from bankruptcy and a home foreclosure.

"When I discovered in early 1985 that the Silva Method Basic Lecture Series was coming to Edmonton, I scrambled to raise the necessary tuition fee. I did not have enough money to feed my family, but I borrowed the fee anyway and attended my first lecture.

"Only two objects were on my mind to solve: Go through bankruptcy in a short period (average eight to twelve months), and buy my house back from the bank that foreclosed on me.

"Within sixty days of completing the Basic Lecture Series, I had repurchased my home with 100 percent financing from the very bank that had foreclosed at three percent *below* the current rates at that time. This had never been done before in this fashion with any Canadian bank.

"I also got through my bankruptcy in a record four months.

"I used the simple but powerful Silva Method technique of visualizing achievements on my mental screen in the above cases.

"One of my most memorable achievements in sales using the Silva Method occurred in the early part of 1988. I had had an expensive acreage ($300,000) for sale for approximately ten months and decided to put some effort into selling it. I used my mental screen and mentally pictured myself putting a sold sign on the property numerous times.

"That's it, just imagining myself putting up the sold sign. Within forty-five days a call came in from someone who had seen the For Sale sign on the property. It was the first call in months. Not many buyers existed for this kind of property and any call was welcome.

"The price did not deter the buyer and he'd seen the property so there was a reasonable possibility that he could actually buy it, and buy it he did! However, a problem existed in that he had to sell his own home first. Normally that wouldn't be a problem except that his was an acreage in the very same subdivision, valued in the $150,000 range—again, not an easy task to complete.

"Here I'd solved one problem only to create another. I was in quite a dilemma. But at least something was happening, so I kept programming.

"I realized I had not been specific enough in selling the expensive home and would need to be much more accurate on the less-expensive acreage. Off to work I went, using my mental screen.

"I only needed to work on the second property, for the sale of it would complete the sale of the larger one automatically. I mentally pictured a number of things, as follows (in no particular order):

"First, standing in front of the property with a prospect, discussing it.

"Second, showing the interior and having the buyer nod his head positively often. He, or they, liked it.

"Third, writing an offer.

"Fourth, presenting the offer. The asking price was $155,000, and I imagined the selling price to be $150,000, all cash. I imagined a deposit of $10,000 to show seriousness, and a possession date soon enough to allow my commission payout to go on an important trip. I expected this to be a no-conditions offer, indicating an immediate sale. It is best not to put a time limit on your programming unless it is necessary. In this instance, I considered it necessary because of the importance of the trip I wanted to make.

"Fifth, putting up a sold sign on both properties.

"Sixth, collecting the commission.

"I also decided that I would throw myself a curve and add something that would challenge me mentally and test my Silva skills and beliefs. That challenge was to say that the buyer of this home would be from out of the country. Not only are there few buyers for this type of property, but the vast majority of acreage buyers come from the general area, and certainly not from out of the country. This was to be a true test.

"A few weeks after I started I held an open house for the public. It was advertised well and the weather was excellent. The response was good both days, but at the end of the second day, no solid buyers.

"Then in came a couple who fell in love with the home

on the spot. We started to discuss a purchase but a few ingredients needed to be added. Money was one of them, but I felt it was solvable. They wanted to sleep on it and we would talk the following day.

"What was unbelievable about these people was that they were Californians who had been transferred to Edmonton. Were these my out-of-country buyers? As it turned out they weren't, so I went back to my mental screen and continued programming. All the signs pointed to the fact that I was making progress on this project.

"Soon another caller expressed interest in an ad I'd placed. He had to call me three times because, for some strange reason, my messages from him had been lost. After some preliminary questions from him, he decided to take a look.

"We met at the property, stood in front as I had imagined, and walked in. Throughout the showing he was positive, and after seeing a few more homes over the next few days, he decided to make an offer.

"I was ecstatic about the whole situation because everything seemed to fall in place. Here's what happened:

"He purchased the property for exactly what I had pictured: $150,000.

"His deposit was $20,000, better than the $10,000 I had imagined.

"Possession date was *before* the date I had needed for my trip, to give me enough money to make the trip and enjoy myself.

"There were no conditions on the offer, which meant two properties were sold, making many people happy. It was at least a win-win-win-win situation: both buyers, me, and the people I visited on my trip.

"But what overshadowed all of the above was that the buyer was from out of the country: He was from the Bahamas.

"The commission payable to me was approximately $18,000.

"The main objective in having it paid by a certain time was to allow me to attend the Silva Method 10-day Ultimate Seminar in Laredo, Texas, in August 1988, taught by José Silva himself. I did indeed attend and experienced one of the greatest learning events of my life.

"This story is only one of many achievements in sales using the Silva Method and I know there will be many more."

SCIENCE PROVES VISUALIZATION'S VALUE

For those who are scientifically inclined, there was a fascinating research project conducted by Cecelia A. Prediger, a Silva Method graduate and physical education instructor at Nyack Junior High School in New York. She wanted to find out more about the effects of mental practice on physical skills.

There have been studies conducted in the past showing a comparison of mental practice to physical practice. A report in the classic book *Psycho Cybernetics* tells about the basketball team where the players who practiced physically improved 24 percent while those who practiced mentally, and did not do any physical practice, improved 23 percent.

But there had never been a study to determine what would happen if someone practiced both physically and mentally. According to Prediger, various observations and reviews conclude that "when mental and physical practices are combined, there is a tendency to do better. However, there is no firm evidence to support this view."

So during October and November of 1987 she decided to get that evidence.

She worked with 120 boys and girls from eleven to thirteen years old. She divided them into three groups of 40, and selected a physical skill to test: They would use the sport of field hockey. All procedures were carefully written out, and the instructors who helped in the project were rotated among the various groups to eliminate any possible bias.

On the first day, each group was tested to see how many

times they could hit a target—a traffic cone. Two of the groups scored a total of 12 hits each, the third group 13.

Then they went through seven days of practice sessions. One group spent five minutes each day on the field, shooting at the traffic cones. A second group spent five minutes sitting in the bleachers, going to level, and imagining that they were shooting at the traffic cones. The third group spent two and a half minutes in the bleachers at level, and two and a half minutes on the field with sticks in hand, shooting at the targets.

What were the results?

The group that practiced physically improved from 13 hits to 22, an improvement of 70 percent. The group that practiced mentally went from 12 hits in the pre-test to 20 hits in the post-test, an improvement of 68 percent.

What about the group that divided their practice? Would they also be in the 68 to 70 percent improvement range? After all, they had the same five minutes' total practice time as the other two groups.' Or would they get some benefits from both, and perhaps improve even more?

Their improvement was more than double either of the other groups.' They improved from 12 hits to 31, an improvement of 160 percent!

It was like using two brains instead of one; using two legs instead of one.

Imagine how you will benefit when you start using your greatest asset—your mind—in this manner. Make up your mind to do it now.

WORLD RECORD PERFORMANCE

And finally, here is how one salesman used visualization to help him set a world record and have his name published in 6.5 million copies of the *Guinness Book of World Records*.

Victor Kovens owns and operates a travel agency in Baltimore, Maryland. He is a good salesman; he helps his clients, and earns a lot of money for doing so. He graduated from the Silva Method Basic Lecture Series in the early 1970s and has used the techniques ever since.

One day while at level he came up with a creative idea that would be fun and, if successful, net him a lot of publicity: get his name into the *Guinness Book of World Records* by flying around the world on commercial airlines in less than two days, faster than anyone had ever done before.

It took Kovens just 47 hours 48 minutes and 7 seconds to complete the 25,000-mile trip. He crossed the equator twice, landed in nine countries, and touched points exactly 180 degrees opposite each other on the globe: Lima, Peru, and Bangkok, Thailand.

Along the way he encountered oversold flights, and a 600-mile aerial detour due to the Vietnam war.

"They've made the rules easier now," Kovens said. "The man who holds the record now only had to go 22,800 miles. When I did it in 1975, I had to go 25,606 miles." Today you can get on the Concorde supersonic jet and circle the globe. But not on May 20, 1975.

"It was a question of visualizing and scheduling," Kovens explained. "I had to figure out which were the best points to hit. Then once I knew that it would work in theory, I had to program to actually get on the flights."

At that time, he was an employee of Trans World Airlines, "so I was flying standby. During the trip, the flight from Madrid to Rome was oversold, so I visualized that there'd be no problems getting on that flight, and we got on the flight."

Kovens had no problems getting through customs or making connections. He used some programming tips he got from Dr. George DeSau, a Silva Method lecturer and research consultant.

Kovens began his flight in Lima, Peru, went to Bogotá, Colombia, to Caracas, to Madrid, Rome, Bangkok, Hong Kong, Tokyo, Los Angeles, and back to Lima. There was one problem: He had to go an extra 600 miles around Vietnam because they were afraid of being shot down, so the plane was an hour late.

"After the flight," Kovens continued, "it was a question of visualizing getting in the Guinness book. I think that was the most important thing. I called the editor of the Guinness book in London, from Los Angeles, to ask him whether I should continue on, and he told me to continue on. Before calling, I imagined the telephone conversation and it was almost a rehearsal, the exact words he said.

"After I was back on the airplane for the last leg back to Lima, Peru," Kovens recalled, "the pilot invited me to come sit in the cockpit. He asked me which direction I wanted to land in Lima, and I told him to land whichever way he thought was fastest and best.

"So thanks to visualizing it, they reproduced my name 6.5 million times."

What were the special programming tips that Dr. DeSau offered Kovens?

"He told me that while I was at my level programming, to act and feel the way I'd feel if I were already in the Guinness book. To imagine actually seeing my name in the book and feel the way I'd feel seeing it there.

"He emphasized desire, belief, and expectancy: strong desire because when you fly for that long with only minimal sleep, you need strong desire."

"He got into some real tight spots, but visualized it and rolled right through," Dr. DeSau said. "He did it the hard way. He was running with a handicap, in terms of the world trying to be against him. The world wouldn't stop just because he was making the flight."

Record Book

This could be the *most important page* in this chapter. All superstar salespeople know the importance of keeping good records. You are a winner, and you will demonstrate it to yourself by recording your progress on this page.

What is the most valuable technique you learned in Chapter 8? _____

How will this technique help you? _____

Why is this important to you? _____

Date used and results: _____

SUCCESSES

Date	Technique Used	Results
_____	_____	_____
_____	_____	_____
_____	_____	_____
_____	_____	_____
_____	_____	_____
_____	_____	_____
_____	_____	_____
_____	_____	_____
_____	_____	_____
_____	_____	_____

9

DEVELOPING YOUR
PERSONALITY & CHARISMA

*José Silva says that the best salesperson he ever knew was
the man who sold a milking machine to a farmer who only
had one cow . . . and took the cow as a down payment!*

Have you ever wondered why it seems so easy for some
people to get results? It seems as though they get a hit every
time they come up to bat. Do they have a magic wand that
they use? Or some special incantation? Is there some kind
of special power that the average person has been deprived
of?

If there is any one key to the superstars' success, it is
that they function at the alpha level with conscious awareness, where they have greater insight, make better decisions, develop more creative ideas, and are more sensitive
to other people—with their minds, they can sense what
other people need without being told.

There are many factors involved with whether we like
people or not, whether we trust them or not, whether we
want to do business with them or not. These are obviously
important to salespeople, because if people do not like you
and trust you, then it will be very difficult for you to sell
them anything.

Think about the kind of person you like to do business
with:

- A person whose clothes are old and dirty, or a person who dresses neatly and appropriately for the circumstances, or a person who wears loud, flashy clothes?
- A person who talks about himself and his problems, or a person who remembers your name, and is interested in you and encourages you?
- Someone who keeps telling you how bad things are, how bad people are, or a person who is optimistic and expects good things for the future?
- A person who is bored with her life and keeps talking about how hard it is to make a living in this business, or someone who is enthusiastic about what they are doing, and who does it well?

You get the idea. Let's take a look now at some of the ways that you can make sure you are making a good impression on people.

Here are seven techniques to help you make a good impression so that people will welcome you back:

DRESS FOR THE OCCASION

There are several excellent books on the market that give you specific guidance on how to dress for success, how to select the colors and shades of color that are best for you.

Does it make a difference? The books give convincing arguments and testimonials that the way you dress directly influences how much money you can make as a salesperson.

There is no one way that is right for everyone. Probably the closest to a sure thing is that men will do better when they wear a tie, in almost any kind of selling.

Sometimes it does not pay to dress too well; your clothes could distract from the message. In some of the glamour industries however, high-fashion designer clothes will help you make more sales.

To determine what is best for you, first study the books

that are available, and consult people who can help you with your appearance. Then, enter your level and at level, make up your own mind about the "look" that is best for you.

When you involve both Wilfred and Willie in the decision, you will come up with the right answer. Remember from time to time to review your decisions at level to see if any changes are indicated.

You can do the same thing to make other decisions about your appearance: hair style, makeup, fragrances, and so forth.

LEARN THE ART OF LISTENING

Everybody loves a good listener. So why is it so hard to do? Each of us is vitally interested in what happens to ourself. It is very flattering to have someone really listen to us.

Joel Howard is a Silva Method graduate in New Jersey who has retired and is now involved with a new venture to manufacture and market specialty electrical cords. He credits the Silva Method techniques with helping him to become a better listener. He has an interesting point: "The better you listen, the better other people hear."

It takes practice to learn to be a better listener. It often takes an effort to learn not to speak for other people. Let the other person finish his or her own statements. And resist the natural tendency to always come up with a story of your own after they stop speaking. It is often good to let the other person have the last word.

It is not our intent to teach you specific techniques to be a good listener. There are people who specialize in that. We will, however, make some suggestions of how to use the alpha level to help you become a better listener.

Go to your level, and at level, recall some of the conversations you had with people today. Did you really listen to what they said? Did you maintain good eye contact with them, and not let your eyes wander while you were thinking about what you were going to say next? Did you make them the hero of the conversation, or were you unconsciously playing one-upmanship? Did you give them time to finish their statements? After they finished speaking, did you wait for a moment before you spoke, or did you rush right in with your own comments?

At level, put yourself on the other side of the table. Imagine that you are the prospect, with your own problems and concerns, with a limited amount of money to spend to solve one of those problems. Then imagine that someone just like you is trying to sell you something. Do you feel that they have your best interest in mind? Do you feel like they really care about whether you solve your problem, or are they just interested in making a sale and earning some money for their own use?

Make up your mind to be a good listener, and program yourself for this goal. After you review your performance on your Mental Screen, erase anything you are not happy with and make a new mental movie the way you want to be. Make up your mind. Desire it. And it is so.

DEVELOPING A SUPERSTAR MEMORY

It has been said that the sweetest sound in the world is the sound of a person's own name.

Your name is something uniquely yours. You have owned it your entire life. If you are like most people, you feel good when people remember your name.

Every politician knows how important it is to remember a person's name. So does every successful salesperson.

It is also important to remember the various likes and dislikes of each customer: their hobbies, the way they like to conduct business, their children that they are so proud of, their achievements.

The first step in developing a great memory for your customers and their interests, is to keep good records. In the old days you would do this with a card file, keeping records on every customer. Now this is easier to do with a data base in a personal computer.

Before going to call on customers, retrieve the information on them and review it. If you make notes immediately after every appointment, then you will have a lot of information for your data base. An easy way is to obtain a small microcassette recorder that you can carry in your pocket, and dictate all relevant information onto the tape, to be transcribed later.

Now, how do you actually remember this information when you get to the customer's office?

Good memory comes from visualization and association.

You can remember better when you recall what something looks like. Think about your home. Can you describe how it looks from the front? If you imagine yourself standing in front of it, what would you see? How tall is it? How wide? What material is it made of? Where is the front door located? Do the windows have shutters? What do they look like? What kind of roof does it have? What material is it made of?

Recalling details like this produces a better memory. You can recall the information you have about your customers in the same manner.

When someone tells you about his or her child who just won first place in a debating contest, imagine what that would look like. If they show you a picture of their offspring, then imagine that child standing in front of an audience, debating other students, and the parents watching. If a customer proudly shows you the golf trophy he just won, study it in detail so that you can easily visualize (recall) him with it later.

When you review your notes about a customer, make mental movies. Recall your last meeting: What were your surroundings when you met with this customer? What did you notice, and comment on? Who stood where, and who did what? Impress these images at your level before your next meeting with your customer.

Get used to thinking about what things look like. If you

already think visually, then practice recalling more details, especially colors. The more you do this, the better your memory will be.

There are several good memory courses on the market, and some excellent books on the subject. We even teach part of a memory course in the Silva Method training, chiefly to help you improve your visualization and imagination so that you will be a better clairvoyant.

Make up your mind to practice recalling scenes and events at your level, to improve your memory and also your visualization and imagination.

HOW TO PROJECT AN AURA OF CONFIDENCE AND SUCCESS

People like to do business with salespeople who are successful, because successful salespeople are those who satisfy their customers' needs. We want our needs to be satisfied, so we want to deal with somebody who satisfies their customers' needs.

Sometimes very successful people do not appear to be successful. They wear old clothes, drive an old car. And sometimes people who have not yet achieved much success appear to be very successful. They wear nice clothes, drive a new car.

We are certainly not advocating that you attempt to deceive people so that you can take advantage of them. One of the things that happens when you start entering alpha every day and practicing the techniques that we are describing, is that your true self emerges, and people that you come into contact with will recognize it.

It is better to program yourself to have a strong desire to help satisfy your customers' needs, than to try to program yourself to merely appear to do so.

It is also a good idea to pay attention to the image you project, to help people see the real you, the one that is there to help satisfy their needs.

José Silva reminds us that we are always consultants, there to help the client find the best way to solve a problem. When you sincerely want to help your customer, and your customer realizes that, then you won't have any competition because nobody else stands a chance.

There are several things you can do to help you project an image of confidence, competence, and concern for your customers' needs.

According to Dave Bellizzi, who has earned several million dollars selling insurance and working as a financial consultant, when you first meet a prospect, there are three steps that they take mentally. "I like you. I trust you. Now I'll listen to what you have to say."

"They initially like you by how you sound on the phone," Bellizzi says. "Analyze your approach at level: How do you come across? Do you waste their time, or get right to the point? Tape record your presentation the next time you call a prospect on the phone, and listen to the tape at level. Listen for the sincerity of your voice, your pace, tone, emphasis.

"When you meet a prospect in person, there are several things to consider. Some people like you by how you look and stand, some by what you say, some by how you play the game. So develop your intuition, so that you can quickly sense the correct approach to use with a prospect. The more you know about your prospect before you get there, the better off you are. Conduct research both at beta and at alpha.

"People like you when they know you are really interested in them," Bellizzi continued. "When somebody tells me only about his product, I don't think he is really interested in me. Let him find out what I want." To do that, of course, the salesperson needs to ask a lot of questions, and be a good listener.

"People want to be treated like they are important, and they are," he continued. "So, look for their noble traits. Remember to treat secretaries nice. With authority, but nice. Don't be too abrupt.

"The way you shake hands, sit in a chair, look in their

eyes, avoid interrupting their train of thought, all makes an impression. Let people talk. They will tell you what they want if you let them talk enough. Then give it to them.''

It is best to avoid arguments. ''My first sales manager told me, 'You can win an argument and lose the sale. It is better to lose the argument and win the sale.'

''People like you when you don't criticize other people's products,'' Bellizzi continued. ''When I first started I thought I had to be better than the competition. Then, I tried something: Just selling my product. That worked so much better. I had no competition! Always say the other guy is good. We are better! Show them how you are better.

''People like you if you are the best at what you do. We all like to deal with the best. Give your qualifications, at the appropriate time. They want to know how long you've been doing it; they want to know if you are qualified to do your job. I keep scrapbooks with all of the clippings about me, and have these in my office. I also have my trophies and awards in my office, to create an aura of success. Of course, if you overdo it, it can backfire. Check it out at your level and decide how much is enough.

''Trust comes from the inside. I know that I would never sell a person a product that wasn't right for them. But I would do everything I could to sell them a product that I know will satisfy their needs.''

NEST MARKETING

Another way to build rapport is rather obvious, but few people think about it: Specialize by selling to people you have a common interest with.

''If you really want to make big money selling,'' Bellizzi explained, ''you've got to speak with thunder. What do I mean by thunder? Conviction!

''People use a phrase, 'He's like one of us.' If you can speak to someone who also has something in common with you, that person will relate to you better, and think, 'Hey, this person is like one of us.'

"If you are twenty-five years old and just getting started in business, you can't really know how a sixty-year-old Chief Executive Officer thinks and feels. Find your own niche, and concentrate there first. Sell to other young adults that you have more things in common with.

"I played college basketball, football, and professional tennis. I speak the 'lingo' of athletes. A lot of my clients are pro athletes. They think I'm one of them.

"I told José Silva that I wanted to design and teach a specialized Silva Method program to athletes and salespeople. Why? I'm an athlete and a salesman. I speak the lingo and understand the problems of these people.

"When you practice this kind of marketing, the prospect feels that, 'This is a person who knows *my* situation. He has been in this business. He knows my problems. I'll trust him.'"

OVERCOME LIMITING BELIEF SYSTEMS

We all have beliefs lurking inside of us that inhibit us from achieving all that we can achieve. But these beliefs are usually hidden from us, because we accept them as being reality instead of just beliefs about reality.

For instance, we know that most businesses have their cycles. There are times of the year that we can make more sales than other times.

S.G., who sells self-improvement seminars, considered April a bad month in his industry, and used to advise new salespeople to be prepared to earn less money that month.

"People have to pay their income taxes in April," he explained, "so they don't have money to spend on seminars." It seems to make sense, doesn't it? People are busy gathering receipts and filling out their income tax returns, so they don't have the time, the money, or the inclination to attend a seminar.

Some of the new salespeople accepted S.G.'s belief, and

sure enough, April was a slow month for them. Other sales-people ignored that advice, and April was one of their biggest months. A lot of people who attend the seminars are people who fill out the short tax form in January and mail it in, and have their tax refund by April. They have some extra money that they can spend, and they are happy to invest it in a seminar that might help them earn more money in the future.

In fact, the Internal Revenue Service says that three out of four people get money back when they file their tax returns.

But S.G. was busy rushing around at the last minute fill-ing out tax forms and scraping up money to pay the extra that he owed, so he was not concentrating on selling sem-inars. When his business dropped, he looked for a handy target to blame it on.

Wilfred will always look for excuses. Wilfred has to have explanations for everything, and he hates to take the blame himself. Willie will tell you the truth. So when you have a temptation to start pointing a finger, notice that there are three other fingers pointing right back at you . . . from your own hand. Go ahead, point at something, and look and see. Even though there might be something out there that influ-ences us, most of the responsibility lies with us.

Enter your level and analyze the situation. Or program a dream to give you guidance. Give Willie a chance, and he will tell you the truth. Then both Willie and Wilfred can help make things better.

"Make good grades if you want to be successful in life." Most of us were told that. So Willie has an association between the grades you made and how successful you will be as a salesperson.

HOW TO PROGRAM TO OVERCOME LIMITING BELIEFS

How can you reprogram that "limiting belief system"?

Enter your level and use your Mental Screen.

Then identify your problem. What is the problem? The

problem is that you are not making enough sales. Perhaps you come right to the close, and then back off and lose the sale. Or maybe you come close to your quota, but stop making appointments for the rest of the month. Something stops you from achieving the results you feel that you should be making.

Visualize that problem on your Mental Screen. You do not need to figure out *why* you have the problem. Just figure out *what* the problem is. Make a good study of it; notice the details. Perhaps as you near your quota, you lose your concentration. Maybe you have more errands to run than usual. Maybe you say the wrong thing when asking for appointments. Study the situation.

Then, erase the problem image from your Mental Screen and create and project a solution image onto your Mental Screen.

What is the solution? The solution is getting the appointments and making the sales. The solution is closing successfully and getting the money.

When you do this, you are giving instructions to Willie to find the cause of the problem and correct it. Perhaps the problem was something that a long-forgotten teacher or coach told you. Perhaps it was a prospect who made you feel so small that you needed a ladder to reach the curb. Maybe it was the way you used to be disappointed at Christmas because somebody else got a better gift than you got.

Whatever it is . . . Willie will deal with it. You may become aware of it, or you may not.

When you program yourself, results are usually permanent.

LEARNS SHE CAN SOLVE PROBLEMS

Sheilah Schwartz went from driving a taxicab in New York City to making million-dollar sales thanks to the Silva Method techniques.

"I was driving the cab on Thirty-ninth Street in Manhattan," she said. "Two girls got in. They were attending the Silva Method training. They said, 'Oh, this is the greatest thing, you've got to take it!' One had taken it the year before, and during that year she was more creative and this and that and what have you."

Sheilah told them that she wanted to open a hair removal business, but could not find the right location. She added that she envisioned it as the biggest in New York. "They told me I definitely had to take the course, and told me about the instructor, June Graham. Three days later, I went."

After learning the Silva Method techniques, she began programming, imagining the perfect location for her electrologist business. "Nothing was materializing at first. I needed a tiny place because I didn't have a lot of money. I envisioned a place, maybe inside a beauty parlor, where I could rent a room or something. I went to all the big ones in New York, but couldn't find anything."

Frustrated, she got a copy of the *Village Voice* newspaper. "Everybody advertises there," she said. "I put my hands over it and said, 'I know you're in there.' The word Gym came into my mind. I called up every place that had anything to do with a gym or exercise. This one studio, when they got on the line, I knew it was the one."

She rented a room from them, started her hair removal business and kept programming. Six months later a new machine came out and she acquired one. Within a few months, she had the biggest hair removal business in New York City.

"Then I panicked," she said. She quit the business.

"I realize now what happened," she explained. "I was brought up to be a failure. I was told I was stupid from the time I understood anything. That was my mother's form of manipulation."

She gave in to the old programming from her childhood. "I decided to sit down and starve to death, unless the universe had something better for me."

One day a friend called. She knew Sheilah had taken an

investment course, and insisted on introducing her to a real estate broker.

"I told her 'I can't sell,'" Sheilah said. "She said, 'Well, you've got nothing better to do, so you are going to go to the office and talk to him.'" They went to Hoboken, New Jersey, to see the realtor. Sheilah still didn't like the idea. "I always thought selling was talking people into buying things. I hate manipulation.

"The way he explained selling was finding the right person for the right thing.

"I thought that was a whole better way to work at it. I thought, I can do that. I thought, Silva built my first business, I'll go back to what works, to Silva.

"I started visualizing sales. My first few months were horrendous. I learned my trade by experience. Then I started visualizing million-dollar sales. I told everybody I was selling million-dollar properties."

People tried to discourage her. "They said there were no million-dollar properties. They pointed out that they had been selling property for twenty years and had never sold a million-dollar property. I told them that was their problem!

"I was canvassing Hoboken, knocking on doors. I had gotten a big button that said, I SOLVE REAL ESTATE PROBLEMS. At this point there was no way I could solve real estate problems. I usually had to go to somebody and ask a lot of questions. That didn't stop me.

"One day a man told me that his girlfriend wanted to sell her building for $1 million. I told him I'd handle it.

"I couldn't get her phone number because it was unlisted. I drove by the building about five times a day for days until I finally found her there. I talked to her, and finished with, 'I'll call you later . . . and your phone number is . . . ?' I told her not to worry about it, she had found the person who was going to make her a millionaire.

"She hung up on me three times before I insisted on coming over and getting that listing. She was an alcoholic. She'd call me at three o'clock in the morning and tell me she was not going to go through with the deal. I stuck with it, and sold it.''

That was the first of many million-dollar deals for Sheilah.

"I would visualize myself going to the closing, and everybody telling me what a great deal I'd put together, and saying, 'Oh, you've solved all the problems.'

"I thought for a while that I might have been causing myself some unnecessary problems, but my Silva Method instructor explained that our job on this planet is to solve problems. The Silva Method doesn't eliminate problems from our life: It teaches us how to solve them. We don't ignore problems and pretend they don't exist. Nor do we dwell on our problems. We identify them, and then we solve them.''

Sheilah has a new project now: helping abused children. "The events that have meant the most to me are the times when I was able to do something to help a child," she explained.

"I am going to be spending some time at level, discussing the problems and seeking solutions," she said. "I am going to do the same thing that I did to build up my real estate business: Program it, and work it.''

A FORMULA TO BOOST YOUR DESIRE

The more you desire something, the harder you will work to get it. All other things being equal, the prize goes to the one who wants it the most. Great coaches and athletes know this, and they know how to motivate themselves and others.

Juan Silva, the Foreign Director for the Silva Method, has developed a powerful motivational formula as a result of nearly forty years of research, practice, and teaching people how to apply the new science of psychorientology.

"Once you make up your mind that you want something," he explains, "then you can increase your desire to get it by going to your level and thinking about it.

"Besides visualizing the solution image that you have created on your Mental Screen, you can increase your desire by thinking of all the reasons you have for reaching your goal.

"If you go to level and think of three reasons for reaching your goal, you will have a certain amount of desire," he explained. "If you keep thinking, and you think of three more reasons for reaching your goal, you will have twice as much desire.

"There are many benefits associated with making a sale. You will benefit, of course. So will your customer. So will your family. So will your customer's family. So will the people you purchase things from with the money you earn.

MOTIVATION TECHNIQUE IN ACTION

"Let me give you an example," he continued. "I recently made a trip to Mexico, and visited the owners of a large factory. I used to manage that factory for them, back in the 1950s. But economic times have been difficult in Mexico, and things have changed.

"We visited the factory, and it was very sad for me to see that much of the large manufacturing facility was sitting idle, with 1,500 of the employees laid off. The manager of the factory is a very good friend of mine. He is a good manager, but the bad nationwide economic conditions had gotten the best of him.

"We left the factory and went to a nearby restaurant to eat lunch. As we talked, my thoughts kept going back to the idle machines in the factory, and to the 1,500 employees who were now out of work and not earning money to support themselves and their families the way they desired.

"I thought about the merchants in town, such as the restaurant where we had come to eat, and how their business would be down since the factory workers had no money coming in. The restaurant should have been crowded during lunchtime, but only a few tables were occupied.

"Many people were suffering. How, I wondered, might I help them? Is there anything I can do to help?

"I asked my friends to excuse me for a moment and I headed towards the rest room. What I wanted, of course, was time to enter my level and think about possible solutions to the problem. The rest room is an excellent place to do this. It is private. It is quiet. Nobody bothers you. And when you close the door, nobody sees you sitting there with your eyes closed.

"When I entered my level, I again thought about all those 1,500 employees who were now out of work. I thought about the empty tables at the restaurant, and the restaurant employees who were now also out of work. I thought about other merchants who were also suffering, along with their families, because of the economic problems.

"Then, after I had completed my study of the problem, I began to think about possible solutions.

"After a few minutes I returned to the table. And I started presenting the ideas that I had thought of at level to the manager of the factory, about where he could find new markets and how he could sell to them.

"The ideas made sense to him. He began to get excited. In fact, he even got me involved by getting me to agree to use some of my contacts in other countries to help him get started.

"'After you came back from the rest room,' the manager told me, 'you did not want to listen to me anymore. You just wanted to tell me your ideas.'

"I agreed. 'That's right. I'd heard all I needed to hear about the problems. I wanted to offer some solutions.'

"'I don't know what you found in that rest room,' my friend said. 'It must have been some kind of think tank, because you sure came back with a lot of good ideas. Thank you for caring.'

"That's the key to the technique I use: I care.

"In order for me to get a strong motivation so that creative ideas for solutions to problems will come, I need to think about all the people who will benefit. In this case, it was not just my friend's son who now manages the factory; it was also the 1,500 employees, their families, and more.

"I had seen things that made me want to help. I had heard the stories of hardship, and I wanted to help. I had imagined what it must be like, and how I would feel if I were in that position and was worried about my employees, their families, and how they must be worried about supporting them, and I wanted to help. I thought about the children of the laid-off employees and how they must have felt, not having new shoes to wear to school, not having money for necessary things, much less extras.

"I had a very strong desire to help, because so many people would benefit.

"Whenever you have that kind of desire to help, and you take action, then you will help solve any problem that exists.

"It is much easier to program for a necessity than for a luxury. And when the need is as urgent, as it was in my friend's factory, then you are almost always guaranteed of success in your programming.

"It will still take a lot of work to build up enough new business to put everyone back to work. It will still take a lot more programming to make the correct decisions, to intuitively sense the needs and how best to fill them. But it can be done.

"When you want to make a sale, think about all of the needs it will satisfy. Think of all of the people who will be better off as a result. When you realize how many people you are helping, then you will make up your mind to make the sale . . . and you *will* make that sale.

"I have always said that if all you do is make a sale and earn a commission, you have not done enough. You should also make a friend. Then you have done your job properly."

Now let's turn the podium over to José Silva again for a technique that he created especially for the Silva Sales Program, to help you gain your prospect's confidence and trust:

A MENTAL TECHNIQUE TO BUILD INSTANT RAPPORT

After you have increased your desire to help your customer, here is a technique that you can use to help convey your inner feelings to your customer.

With this technique, you can communicate with them on an inner level, that you are genuinely there to help them solve a problem, and that what you are selling them is in their best interest.

You cannot use this technique to fool a person into believing you if you are not being truthful. They will know, at an inner level, what your true feelings are. If you want to deceive people, to cheat them and take advantage of them for your own personal gain, then you will be better off not using the Silva Method techniques.

If you sincerely want to help your customers, and you want them to sense this on an inner level, then use this technique:

At night, when you are ready to go to sleep, program yourself to wake up automatically at the ideal time to program yourself with this technique. It is best to do this in a sitting position, with your eyes turned upwards approximately 20 degrees, in the area of your Mental Screen, and your head lowered, or bowed, approximately 20 degrees. After programming yourself to wake up automatically at the ideal time, then lie down and go to sleep from level.

The first time you wake up during the night or in the morning, again sit up in bed, turn your eyes slightly upwards and bow your head slightly, and once again enter your level.

Then pre-program yourself to use the Three Fingers Technique when you are with your prospect or customer. Here is how to proceed:

Bring together the tips of the thumb and first two fingers of either hand, or both hands. Imagine making your pre-

*sentation to your prospect or customer, and imagine bring-
ing together the tips of the thumb and first two fingers of
either hand. Tell yourself mentally that when you are with
your prospect or customer, all you need to do is to bring
together the tips of the thumb and first two fingers of either
hand, as you are doing now, and they will sense that you
are there to help them solve a problem or reach a goal,
that you are there to help them find the solution that is best
for them. Imagine them being receptive to your presentation
and to your ideas; imagine them trusting you as a valued
counselor.*

*Then, if it is not yet time to get up, lie down and go back
to sleep. Then during the day, when you are talking with
your prospect or customer, all you need to do is to bring
together the tips of the thumb and first two fingers of either
hand and expect them to sense that you are telling them
the truth and that they can trust you.*

If you sincerely want to help them, they will sense it.

Record Book

This could be the *most important page* in this chapter. All superstar salespeople know the importance of keeping good records. You are a winner, and you will demonstrate it to yourself by recording your progress on this page.

What is the most valuable technique you learned in Chapter 9? _____

How will this technique help you? _____

Why is this important to you? _____

Date used and results: _____

SUCCESSES

Date	Technique Used	Results
_____	_____	_____
_____	_____	_____
_____	_____	_____
_____	_____	_____
_____	_____	_____
_____	_____	_____
_____	_____	_____
_____	_____	_____
_____	_____	_____

10

SALES PSYCHOLOGY: WHY PEOPLE BUY

A salesman was trying to sell a new state-of-the-art home heating system to an elderly widow. He spent an hour extolling the virtues of the system: the microprocessor controls that made it operate at maximum efficiency, and the space age materials it was made of. He emphasized the twenty-year unconditional guarantee in case it broke. He reviewed the BTU capacity, the minimal space requirements and how easily it could be installed in her home, and all of the ecological advantages of using this particular system.

She nodded politely, but gave no sign that she would buy.

He knew it was perfect for her, and explained once again how it would be the most economical solution to her problem, and would substantially increase the value of her home. Still, she just nodded politely. "Ma'am," he said finally in a resigned voice, "is there anything else I can tell you about this heating system?"

"Just one thing," she said softly.

"Well, please, tell me what that is," he pleaded.

"Will it keep an old lady warm on a cold winter night?"

People buy things because they need them, because they want them, or both.

When you follow certain proven steps, you will be able

to persuade anybody to do anything, as long as it is in their best interest. You can persuade a customer to buy something, you can persuade your children to study, you can persuade your neighbor not to mow his lawn early Sunday morning, you can even persuade your boss to give you a bigger territory or a higher commission—or both.

SALES PSYCHOLOGY

There are certain steps you must take in order to sell something.

First, you must get your prospect's attention. We are all concerned about our own problems, the events in our own lives. You need to break through your prospects' preoccupation with their own problems and arouse their curiosity about your product or service. We discussed this in detail in Chapter 3.

Then you need to find out the reasons why your prospect wants or needs your product or service. We will show you one way to do that in just a moment, and another way in Chapter 14.

Next, you explain how your product or service helps them meet that need. This is when you convince them that your product will do the job for them.

Tell them why it is important to make a decision now. Work on their desire to get the benefits of your product or service *now*.

Then close the sale.

FIND YOUR CUSTOMER'S REAL NEEDS

Would you like to make a living trying to sell people something they don't want or care about, or would you rather earn your living selling people something that they need, want, and desire?

When you find out what your customers want, and show

them how your product or service will help them get it, then selling is easy and fun.

There are two ways that you can find out what your customers really want:

- Objective—asking them questions and listening to their answers.
- Subjective—using your mind at the alpha level to sense what they really want. We will cover that in Chapter 14.

Right now, let's see how asking questions can help both you and your customer uncover their real desires.

People don't always know what they really want.

Most people, for instance, think that they want money. But money is not what they really want; they only want money as a means to get them what they really want.

Silva Method lecturer and research consultant Dr. George DeSau was once told by a woman attending the Silva Basic Lecture Series with him that she wanted money.

Dr. DeSau reached in his pocket, got out a penny and gave it to her.

"No," she said, shaking her head, "I want more money than that."

Dr. DeSau again reached into his pocket, pulled out a dime, and gave it to her.

That still did not satisfy her. "I want a lot more money than that," she said.

So Dr. DeSau took out his wallet, pulled out a $5 bill, and handed that to her. "There, that's a lot more than the penny and the dime," he said. "Are you satisfied now?"

"No!" she said.

"Then perhaps you should be more specific," Dr. DeSau suggested.

"I want $80,000," she replied.

Dr. DeSau folded his wallet and put it back in his pocket. Then he asked her, "Why do you want $80,000?"

"To buy a house," she answered.

"So what you really want is not the money, but a house?" Dr. DeSau probed.

"Yes, that's right," she agreed. She even described the house to him.

Another Silva Method lecturer, Bill Ricke, told that story in a Silva Method class. When he finished a man spoke up. "I know of a situation exactly like that," he said.

Ricke asked him to elaborate.

"I know a woman who found herself in a position of having a little income but no cash after her husband died," he explained. "She wanted to purchase an $80,000 house. But she did not have the money for the down payment.

"However," he continued, "she had an antique automobile that her husband had restored. The owner of the house had always wanted a car like that, and was willing to accept it as a down payment. She got financing for the balance of the purchase price, and moved into her house without any money changing hands."

A SIMPLE QUESTION TO HELP YOU FIND THE REAL GOAL

Often, all you have to do to learn what your customer really wants, is to ask them.

Do just what Dr. DeSau did: Ask them *why* they want whatever it is they are asking about.

"Find out *why* they need your product or service," Dave Bellizzi says. "Then explain how your product or service helps them meet that need. After you have reached agreement with them on those two points, then tell them why it is important to make a decision *now*. Then close the sale."

This is one of the best ways you really can help your customer. Remember what José Silva said about the value of being a consultant to your customers. Help them clarify what they really want, and you can do a better job of satisfying their needs.

"Why do you want a new car?" If the answer is reliability so the wife and children will be safer, then talk to them about safety and reliability, because that's what they are really buying.

"Why do you want a new home?" Perhaps they are looking for a better neighborhood, or to be close to a better school for their children. Maybe they want to provide their children with the nice, clean home with the spacious yard that they never had when they were growing up. Learn what their real goals are, and help them even more.

"Why do you want to earn additional income?" If they tell you that they need it so they can send their daughter to college, then you have discovered what *really* motivates them, and you are in a better position to help them get what they *really* want.

Before you start talking about your product, get your prospects to talk about themselves first. This helps break down sales resistance. People like to talk about themselves. After they do, they feel obligated to listen to you.

You can make a transition from talking about them to talking about your product by saying, "Okay, I know you're busy, so I'll get right down to business."

As you develop your intuitive abilities as explained in Chapter 14, you will be better able to uncover their real desires even when they are being evasive and not opening up to you.

Remember, you can program yourself to have better rapport with someone. In Chapter 9 José Silva explained exactly how.

HOW TO INCREASE YOUR WORTH TO YOUR CUSTOMERS

Ana Maria Mendez asked, during a Silva Method Sales Training Seminar, how this would apply to her business: selling encyclopedias door to door.

"What you are selling is an encyclopedia," the instructor answered. "Why is an encyclopedia important for the children in this family?'' ''They will make better grades which will help them later to get better jobs and earn more money'' she replied. ''You are not selling them books, but a better life for their children,'' the lecturer pointed out.

The radio advertising sales rep is not just selling airtime, or even increased income for the business. To determine what the businessperson is buying, ask why the increased income is important. Does the business owner want to expand the business, or prepare for retirement, or send the kids to college?

''Usually, when someone speaks of earning additional income, they have it sort of mentally earmarked for some specific purpose, and you probably do too. Would you share with me what that purpose is?'' Ask them that question. The answer will tell you what they already desire.

One very important note here: You have to establish the right environment for asking that kind of question. If you spring it on a person before they are ready, you will probably not get your answer.

How do you create the right environment to ask personal questions?

It is very simple.

Just ask for permission:

''In order to help determine what fits your needs and what's in your best interest, may I ask you a few questions?'' When they agree, then you can easily get any information that you need.

Very few salespeople care enough about their customers to learn what they like and dislike, what their hopes and dreams are. And many of those who do ask those questions do so only to use the answers as additional ammunition to make the sale.

Keep in mind that when you ask your prospects Why they want something, you are helping them clarify their goals. Even if they never purchase anything from you, they are better off as a result of having talked with you.

Isn't that a great feeling? How could you ever feel uncertain about making cold calls, about asking for appointments, about spending time with a prospect to show them your product, when you know that as a result, the prospect is always going to be better off than they were before?

A $5,000 THANK YOU

When he isn't busy teaching salespeople how to increase their sales, Dennis Higgins manages several businesses, one a welding business in Corpus Christi, Texas.

One fall afternoon a man came in and asked, "How much will you charge to build me a gate?"

Dennis began asking questions, and learned that it would be a gate for the entrance to his father's ranch.

"I have priced gates at other shops," the man said. "They can make me a nice one for about $2,000."

"Well, I could build you one for that," Dennis agreed. "Can I ask you something else? Why are you buying the gate at this particular time?"

The man became very emotional. "My father is terminally ill," he said. "It is not likely that he will ever see another Christmas. I've never been able to tell him how much I love him. I want to do this to show him how much I love him before it's too late."

What would you do after learning that?

Dennis pointed out that the way to show his real love for his father was not by buying the cheapest gate he could get, but by buying the best he could afford. The sale came to $5,000.

They even arranged a special time to put the gate up, while the family took their father to Houston for treatment. Then when they returned, they drove to the ranch and surprised him with the new gate. The son was finally able to show his father how grateful he was and how much he really loved him.

EXPLAIN HOW YOUR PRODUCT HELPS THEM MEET THEIR NEED

Remember that people buy for their own reasons. You may know that your product will save them a great deal of money, but if they are buying it for the prestige value, that is what you emphasize to them.

After you know what your customer wants to buy, then it is time to present, show, explain or demonstrate how your product is the best product to meet that need, to satisfy that desire, to solve that problem. Build your presentation around the answer to the Why question.

Whenever you explain a *feature* of your product, you *must* mention a *benefit* that meets one of your customer's needs. Then you can use a trial close.

Right now, let's explain the difference between features and benefits:

The refrigerator (product) has a ten-year guarantee (feature) so if anything goes wrong, we'll pay for the repair (benefit).

Then use a trial close to measure your customer's interest at this point: That's important to you, isn't it? (trial close).

Here's another example:

This car (product) has a five-speed transmission (feature) that will help you save money on gas, which you can then put into a savings account for your daughter's college education (benefit). That is what's really important to you, isn't it?

During this phase of your presentation, use testimonials if you can. Tell them about your company. Doing this will help build credibility and reassure them that they are dealing with somebody who is reputable and will deliver what is promised.

Use whatever tools you have available for your particular product to help you make an effective presentation.

Demonstrations are very effective for some products.

Show how just one drop of this superior cleaning fluid removes the stain completely. Automobile dealers know the value of letting a client drive a new car around the block . . . or even to their home where all the neighbors will see it.

Sometimes visual aids will help you sell your product. You can use anything from printed pictures, charts and graphs, to slides and video productions to show people how your product works, what it has done for other people, what it looks like in action. Videos are a good way to show testimonials.

The telephone can be a powerful tool for you to use. Imagine a prospect who is on the fence, who hasn't quite decided to buy or not. You ask if you can borrow their phone for a moment, and call a satisfied customer. Then ask your customer if he or she will speak to your prospect about the quality of your product, the caliber of your service, the benefits received, the money saved. This is very powerful if your satisfied customer is in the same business as your prospect.

FAN THE FLAME OF THEIR DESIRE

During your questioning you learned what your prospect really wants. When you asked them why they would be interested in your product or service, they told you what they really desire.

Remind them of this just before you ask them to buy.

"The ten-year guarantee on this refrigerator will give you peace of mind, because you will know you will not have any additional costs. That is what you want, isn't it?"

"I can assure you, Mr. Prospect, that you will love the way this car saves you money on your gasoline bills, so that you can put it into the savings account for your daughter's education. That is what you want, isn't it?"

Remind them of why they want the product or service, and mention how your product or service will give them that special benefit that is so important to them.

Then you are ready to move into the action phase, the close.

We will cover closing in Chapter 12. In Chapter 11, we will show you some more strategies for preparing the way so that closing will be easy and natural.

CREATING A SUPER POWER PRESENTATION

You can create a super power sales presentation for yourself by spending time at your level, reviewing and analyzing your sales presentations to see how you can improve what you are doing.

Develop a strong attention getter.

Then determine your prospect's specific needs by asking questions. All you have to do is ask them, and they will tell you what they are willing to buy. Learn to listen. If you let people talk long enough, they will tell you what they want. Then convince them that your product or service will help them get what they really desire. We will discuss this more in the next chapter.

After that, ask for the order. Ask when they want it delivered, or if they are paying by check or credit card, or any other appropriate question. It is your responsibility to help them make the right choice and take action. If you don't, they will miss out. Have the courage to accept this responsibility. When you know that you are helping them, it will be easy.

You can program yourself with your Mental Screen and your Three Fingers Technique to remember the correct steps to take to make a sale, and then to do what your customer needs.

Record Book

This could be the *most important page* in this chapter. All superstar salespeople know the importance of keeping good records. You are a winner, and you will demonstrate it to yourself by recording your progress on this page.

What is the most valuable technique you learned in Chapter 10? _____

How will this technique help you? _____

Why is this important to you? _____

Date used and results: _____

SUCCESSES

Date	Technique Used	Results
_____	_____	_____
_____	_____	_____
_____	_____	_____
_____	_____	_____
_____	_____	_____
_____	_____	_____
_____	_____	_____
_____	_____	_____
_____	_____	_____
_____	_____	_____

11

MAKING THE DEAL

Two salesmen, Tom and Jerry, were hiking in the mountains one Saturday when they spotted a bear foraging for food. Simultaneously, it seemed, the bear spotted them and turned and started walking in their direction.

"Look at that bear!" Tom said. "I wonder what he eats?"

Jerry, who prided himself on always having all the facts about everything, said, "Some bears prefer berries and honey, but that species is carnivorous."

"What does that mean?" Tom asked. Jerry always suspected that Tom wasn't too bright. He thought Tom should spend more time studying and learning facts. Tom preferred to spend his time listening to his customers and figuring out new ways that they could benefit from his product.

"Carnivorous means that the bear eats meat," Jerry said.

"And I suppose that includes people?"

"Yes, it does," Jerry answered.

"There are no trees nearby," Tom observed. "We'd better run."

Then Jerry began to lecture Tom: "That bear can run twenty miles an hour, and his legs are so powerful that he can accelerate faster than a human being. So there is no point in trying to outrun him."

Tom quickly sat down, took off his hiking boots, got his sneakers out of his backpack, and started putting them on.

"Why are you doing that?" Jerry asked, annoyed. "I just explained to you that you can't outrun that bear."

"I don't have to outrun the bear," Tom answered. "All I have to do is outrun you!"

It is not just what you know, but how you use it that will make you a superstar. You can take all the sales courses in the world and they won't make you a superstar salesperson unless you know how to use your mind the special way you are learning now, to apply what you know.

Sometimes it seems like the sales interview is a battle of wits as you try to keep up with the prospect. Think about it: None of us really likes to part with our money until we are absolutely certain that we are buying something that we really want. We certainly don't want to be embarrassed by spending our money foolishly, on things that don't satisfy our basic wants and desires.

The closer the prospect is to buying, the harder he or she will strive to come up with reasons for not buying. If they hear any "rustling in the bushes," anything that they are not certain of, anything that they do not fully understand, then the flight or fight mechanism will kick in and they will run . . . away from the sale.

Let's look at some ways that we can use cooperation rather than confrontation to make more deals.

SELL BENEFITS, BENEFITS, BENEFITS

Always remember this: Benefits sell products. How will your product or service benefit your customer and get them what they want?

A piece of information about your product or service is known as a feature. When you tell a prospect that the electric drill you want to sell him rotates at a speed of 2,000 revolutions per minute, you have given him a feature.

What does that mean to him? Why is that an advantage to him?

When you tell him that this means it will drill cleaner holes, or drill holes faster, you are talking about benefits.

As you learned in the last chapter, you can carry benefits a step farther when you know *Why* it is important to them.

"This investment pays higher interest." Is that a feature or a benefit? It is a feature of course. Why does this particular customer want higher interest? Find the answer to that question, and then you can sell them on your investment opportunity.

The product is a microwave oven. A feature is that it will cook your food faster. A benefit is that it will save you time.

The product is a fax machine. A feature is that it is a faster way to send documents to a distant location. A benefit is that decisions can be made more quickly.

The product is insurance. A feature is how much it pays. Benefits are peace of mind and security.

This even works for selling books. Bob Stone, who has authored more than eighty self-improvement books, including several about the Silva Method (some co-authored with José Silva) tells how: In the introduction, he says, list the benefits the person will get from reading the book. Tell them what they will learn by reading the book, and what they have to do to get the benefits. As an example, check the introduction to this book.

To make it easier to understand, let's give examples of how several salespeople have profited by selling benefits.

OVERCOMING THE PERFECT OBJECTION

How can a telephone solicitor sell a subscription to a large daily newspaper to a blind woman?

That was the challenge that one day faced a man whom we shall call Joe Thompson.

What did he do? He looked for benefits. He had to—the

features of his product worked against him in this instance.

Thompson told her about all the news in the *News*, and she said that she would like to know the news. He told her about all of the special and regular features, and she liked those too. The same with the advertising, with the special sales and discount coupons.

But there was one problem: She was completely blind. And she was becoming depressed thinking about all that she was missing.

Thompson asked if there was anyone there who could read the paper to her.

No, she lived alone.

What about friends who came to visit, would they spend a little time reading the paper to her?

She told Thompson that people used to come visit her, but lately it was rare for anyone to pay her a visit. In fact, she was very lonely, and could not even pass the time with the newspaper because, of course, she was blind. It seemed that she was missing out on everything in life.

This was getting more depressing by the minute.

But Joe Thompson is very good at thinking about benefits. So he thought, What does this woman need more than anything else, and how can my product—the daily newspaper—help her to get it?

It was obvious to Thompson. She was old, blind, and lonely. What she needed the most was to have people visit her every day. Now, how could a newspaper subscription help make that happen?

"Do people have a reason to visit you?" he asked.

She answered No.

"Maybe," he said, "they don't visit you because they don't have any specific reason to visit. Perhaps if they knew that you got the paper every day, then your friends would take turns coming to visit you and read the paper to you."

She liked the idea, and told Thompson to enter a subscription for her.

Thompson checked up on her from time to time over the next several months. People were coming to visit her every day. They would read the paper, and would discuss together the items they had read. The blind woman was happier than she had been in years, all because a salesman who cared took the time to find out what she really wanted and helped her solve a problem.

WON OUT OVER UNBEATABLE COMPETITION

There is real magic in caring about your prospects and customers. Consider some of the stories that Frank Bettger tells in his classic book, *How I Raised Myself from Failure to Success in Selling* (Prentice-Hall, 1949).

There are two points to be made by his stories; Bettger recognized and explained one, and José Silva uncovered the other during his research into how the mind works.

Bettger was a young man trying to get started selling life insurance. He was not very successful, he admits.

Then he tells of a couple of incidents that changed his whole attitude about selling. He learned that "The most important secret of salesmanship is to find out what the other fellow wants, then help him find the best way to get it."

By way of illustration, Bettger tells about how he approached the owner of a wholesale grocery about buying some life insurance. The grocer abruptly told Bettger that he was near retirement, his children were all grown and well taken care of, and he had all the insurance he needed. It appeared that this man didn't need any insurance.

Then Bettger had a hunch and asked a question. He asked the man about outside interests, especially charities. Had the man ever considered, Bettger inquired, that when he died, the charities would no longer receive the donation from him? That eventually led to the sale of several insurance policies, with the proceeds to go to the charities after the merchant's death.

Bettger's book is worth reading. When you read it keep one thing in mind: He was using a special mental ability to help him obtain information. He admits that he "took a blind stab, and accidentally found what (the merchant) wanted."

José Silva's research revealed that some people, only about 1 in 10, somehow grow up with the ability to sense information with their minds. We are all very creative and intuitive when we are young. But as we grow up, most people become more and more involved in the physical world and its pleasures; 9 out of 10 people develop their reasoning ability, and learn to depend on facts and logic, but lose that creative, intuitive side of their nature.

Only a very few keep that creative, intuitive ability that we are all born with. Wilfred gets so loud that Willie can no longer be heard.

Frank Bettger, like José Silva and many other super successful people, had little formal education. Bettger never finished grade school. He was an athlete, and had played professional baseball. Most successful athletes become successful at least in part because they have great anticipation. Another way you could say that is, that they have great intuition.

From all indications, Frank Bettger was one of the natural alpha thinkers, who could use both brain hemispheres to think with. He was a natural clairvoyant, who could hear both Wilfred and Willie.

Another story seems to confirm this. Bettger traveled to New York City to make a presentation to a large manufacturer who was in the market for a sizable life insurance policy. The manufacturer's company was borrowing money for expansion, and the lenders wanted a policy on his life to cover the loan.

Ten large companies had already submitted proposals, Bettger said, including three from agents who were long-time personal friends of the manufacturer.

Bettger asked the manufacturer why he had not made the acquiring of that insurance his top priority. If he failed the medical exam, he would not get the insurance, and therefore not get the loan, Bettger pointed out. What could be more important to your company, he asked.

Then Bettger told the prospect that he had made an appointment for that morning with the only doctor in New York whose examination would be sufficient for the insurance companies to issue the policy immediately, without confirmation from another physician. Why wait? Bettger asked.

The manufacturer thought about it, then asked Bettger who he represented. "I represent you!" Bettger answered. After a few minutes more thought, they went to the doctor, passed the exam, and got the insurance.

How did Bettger come up with that idea? He explains in his book what he did as he sat at his desk the night before. "For half an hour my mind just ran around in circles," he recalls. "Then some questions began to pop—questions that should help this man crystallize his thinking and aid him in making a decision."

You will enjoy reading the whole story. Just remember when reading Bettger's book, or books from any of the super successful who tell how they did it, that they are natural alpha thinkers. The ideas that come to them, come from the prospect's mind. They are able to sense ahead of time what the prospect needs.

If your mind doesn't function this way, you can learn how. You must learn directly from someone whose mind functions this way. It takes a mind to train another mind. My Wilfred can educate your Wilfred, and either one of us can have our Wilfred talk to your Willie. But only a trained Willie can train another Willie.

Chapter 14 explains the process in more detail, and shows you exactly how you can proceed to develop this ability. At the end of this chapter, José Silva will show you a technique that you can start using immediately to be more sensitive to your customers, so that you will know what to say to best serve their needs and make the sale.

The saddest thing about most of the self-improvement and how-to books on the market is that they were written by or about the super successful alpha thinkers, and none of them realize that 90 percent of the people who read the book cannot function the same way they do. Most people cannot sit at their desk and actually sense their prospect's needs; they cannot take a blind stab and come up with the right answer.

HOW A NATURAL PSYCHIC FUNCTIONS

Jeff Herman is an example of a natural psychic who uses his creative and intuitive ability to serve his clients better. He is an author's agent, and he is rapidly building a reputation as one of the best in the very competitive New York City market.

One of Jeff's clients is Edward J. Rogers, author of *Getting Hired: Everything You Need to Know About Résumés, Interviews and Job Hunting Strategies.* It struck Herman that if there ever was a premium for corporations to give away to graduating college students, *Getting Hired* was it.

Time magazine bought a few thousand copies to distribute along with its student subscriptions.

Herman thought it was worth more than that. So he proposed to several corporations that they buy the book in very large quantities, customize it with their own logos, and distribute them free to college students. The highest bidder was the Adolph Coors Company. They bought 164,750 copies to give away free on college campuses. That was just the first year.

When asked how he came up with that idea, Herman answered without hesitation: "I don't know."

When asked when creative marketing ideas come to him, he thought for a moment. "When I'm walking," he said. "Or when I'm driving, or taking the subway. Usually when I'm in between something."

His answer demonstrates the difference between the 10 percent of humanity who develop their intuition through natural means, and those who learn a standardized system to use their intuition.

The "naturals" often have to wait for it to happen. Even though they are blessed with the ability to get help from the other side, they cannot always do it on demand.

People who have developed their intuitive ability through the Silva Method techniques can make it happen, anytime they desire.

Silva Method graduates can take time out, find a quiet place (such as a rest room), enter their level, and have an answer within a matter of minutes.

The good news is that the "naturals" can learn the Silva Method techniques just like everyone else. And since they are already accustomed to using their intuition, they make great progress quickly.

Oh, yes, one more thing about Jeff Herman: At a time when publishers were saying that sales books wouldn't sell, Jeff Herman and Rena Wolner, an editor at Putnam, were intuitive enough to know that this one would. Were they right? There have already been enough advance orders to justify their judgment.

OVERCOME OBJECTIONS BY AGREEING WITH THEM

Sales psychorientology emphasizes cooperation rather than confrontation. You have seen that throughout this book.

What about objections?

When a prospect comes up with an objection, the natural tendency is to show that they are wrong, and that you are right. That would destroy the whole mood of cooperation that you have worked so hard to create. You are representing the prospect, and seeking the best possible solution for the prospect. You do not want to spoil that by getting into an argument, or even by hinting that they don't know what's best for them.

So when they come up with an objection, agree with them. Then come up with a solution that is satisfactory to both of you.

One word of caution here: Avoid the word "But." When you use "But," you immediately stop things. "Yes, I agree with you, but . . . '' See how that changes direction completely? Think about it; usually when we hear the word "But" it is like running into a brick wall. "I agree with you, but . . . you are wrong!"

Instead of saying "But," just end your sentence, pause a moment, and start a new sentence and say what you want to say.

"Yes, Option B would be a good choice. Our research has shown that many people prefer Option A for these reasons . . . '' If you begin the second sentence with the word "But," you throw up an unnecessary obstacle.

In a moment, we will call on José Silva to give us a special mental technique to help accomplish that. First, let's see how this works in action.

DENNIS HIGGINS OVERCOMES A KILLER OBJECTION

Objections can come at any time. Usually the harshest cries come when you are closest to consummating the sale. Nobody wants to spend money unwisely, so most prospects come up with every objection they can think of, no matter how unreasonable.

Sometimes the objections come after the deal has been made. These objections can kill a deal just as quickly as any other objections unless you handle them correctly.

Dennis Higgins had just such a situation recently. Here's the situation and how he handled it:

"I had reached an agreement with a developer for our company to fabricate some items for him. I agreed that we would paint and deliver the items to him by a certain date for a price of $15,000. The developer agreed, and I went back to my office to write up a contract.

"When I returned to his office, which was located at the top of a beautiful high-rise building overlooking the city of Corpus Christi, he had a surprise for me. 'We just want to add in a one-year guarantee on the paint job,' he told me.

"My first inclination was to fight. What did he mean changing our agreement. I had entered into it in good faith, and had given him a very good deal. I would make a profit, but I certainly wasn't taking advantage of him. I really wanted to tell him that I understood how he might want that, but that what he was doing was not very ethical. I didn't say it. I held my temper and my tongue.

"Instead, I took a deep breath and relaxed. I defocused my vision and recalled the feeling of being at level. And I brought together the tips of the thumb and first two fingers of my hand, and wondered what to say next. How would I handle this? I took another deep breath, and spoke.

" 'That's a very good point,' I said. 'It shows that you know your business.' I wanted to agree with him, and not get into an argument that could cost me the sale, and could cost him the excellent work he could get from us at an excellent price. We would both lose if I lost my temper. I was very careful not to use the word 'But.'

"My answer appeared to take him by surprise. He probably expected me to argue or cry or something, anything but agree with him. I continued:

" 'To tell the truth,' I said, 'I am glad that you have reopened negotiations, because there are a couple of other factors that I would like to include in the contract before we sign it.'

" 'What do you mean other factors?' he asked sharply. 'Are you talking about charging me more?'

" 'Well,' I answered, 'we just got word from one of our suppliers that he is increasing his prices, effective immediately . . . '

" 'But we have a deal,' the developer said.

" 'Yes, that's true,' I agreed. 'Now let me get this straight, did you want to renegotiate that deal, or did you want me to sign it the way we agreed on yesterday?'

" 'I want you to sign it right now,' he said. 'Are you willing to do that?'

"I told him that he was right and I would stick with the original arrangement. We both signed the contract. He was completely satisfied with the work we did for him, and has hired us several more times since then.''

Now let's turn the podium over to José Silva to show us how to use mental techniques to deal with difficult situations and make more sales.

STRATEGIES TO HELP YOU MAKE MORE SALES

Here is a technique that you can use to get information clairvoyantly, even if you are not one of the 10 percent who have naturally developed the ability to function clairvoyantly with conscious awareness and control.

Actually, you have already learned: Dream Control.

Once you have practiced Dream Control Steps 1 and 2, to develop your ability to remember and interpret your dreams, you can then program to have a dream that will contain information to help you solve the problem that you have in mind. You can review Chapter 7 for complete details.

While you are sleeping, your brain frequency cycles back and forth all night long, like the ebb and flow of the tide. Approximately every ninety minutes, it goes from low beta all the way to deep delta.

During this time, Willie can scan your brain cells for any appropriate information to help you solve the problem.

While at the alpha level, Willie can get information from Will, that Will can obtain from anyone's brain cells, anywhere in the world.

In other words, you can obtain information clairvoyantly while you sleep. When you develop Dream Control Step 3, you can become aware of this information in your dreams.

When you have a proposal to make, program a dream to give you guidance. The more you practice, the more successful you will be with this technique.

There is another technique that you can use on the spot, when you are face to face with a client and need to come up with immediate answers: the Three Fingers Technique.

You have already learned how to pre-program yourself to use the Three Fingers Technique to help you in several different ways. You can also pre-program yourself with the Three Fingers Technique to help you come up with the best response to objections, for instance.

You can review how to pre-program yourself with the Three Fingers Technique in Chapter 5.

When you are within range of a person's aura—the electromagnetic and other radiations that a person emits—then you can learn to be sensitive to their moods and feelings. Once you develop this sensitivity, then you will have more information to work with in determining how to respond to them and make the sale.

This is not the same as the techniques we discuss in Chapter 14, but by developing these techniques, you will be even more effective with those in Chapter 14.

Record Book

This could be the *most important page* in this chapter. All superstar salespeople know the importance of keeping good records. You are a winner, and you will demonstrate it to yourself by recording your progress on this page.

What is the most valuable technique you learned in Chapter 11? _____

How will this technique help you? _____

Why is this important to you? _____

Date used and results: _____

SUCCESSES

Date	Technique Used	Results
_____	_____	_____
_____	_____	_____
_____	_____	_____
_____	_____	_____
_____	_____	_____
_____	_____	_____
_____	_____	_____
_____	_____	_____
_____	_____	_____

12

CREATIVE CLOSING

Everything was going well forty-five minutes into an important sample talk for a big sales company. On the line was a big training contract and the boss, who was an old experienced hand at selling, the man who would write the check, was watching grimly from the back of the room.

"We have fifteen minutes left, teach them how to close," *he said. I could almost perceive a smile at the corners of his mouth.*

Only fifteen minutes left! This was definitely a test.

Enter the Silva Method.

I relaxed, took a deep breath, and the idea "popped" right into my head.

"Please send to the front of the room the person in your company with the least amount of sales experience," *I asked.*

A chuckle went through the crowd and they produced an eighteen-year-old high school graduate hired to do some filing. The boss called out, "And she has absolutely no sales experience!" He was beaming.

"We're at the end of the sale," *I said, "and everything hangs in the balance. It could go either way. In a moment she will tell me something about your product and I will whisper into her ear the 'secret of closing sales.'"*

A tiny, quaking voice said, "Buy this thing and you'll save money."

I leaned forward and whispered the secret in her ear. She thought for a moment and said, "All we have to do is get some information. Where do you want them delivered?"

"Can anyone guess what I just told her?" I asked. A barrage of the usual "sales speak" followed. No one had the answer.

"Give us another chance? Let us try again."

So we gave them another chance.

"Buy this product and you'll be happy you did," she said with more confidence. I leaned forward and whispered the secret again.

"Okay," she said, "did you want one of these or two?" More confidence now. She was on a roll!

The guesses were coming fast now. What could she have learned that all the "experienced" closers didn't know?

"Would you tell the people in the audience the secret," I asked her, "the age-old secret of closing sales that I whispered in your ear."

She shrugged her shoulders. "All he whispered was, 'Okay, I'll take it, what do we have to do?'"

A hundred stunned faces stared up at us. From the back of the room, a belly laugh and a big smile told me that the sale was mine.

You may be sitting there right now thinking to yourself that closing can't be that easy. But the truth is, once you understand the process, closing is just about that easy.

WHY PEOPLE BUY

Remember when we talked earlier about why people buy? People buy on emotion. People buy on desire. You learned in Chapter 10 how to learn what people desire, what they get emotional about.

Once you know what a prospect really desires, and you

connect your product to their desire by showing them how your product will help them get what they desire, then they are ready to buy. They want to reach that goal; they have a good mental image of that goal; mentally they already possess that goal; now it is up to you to deliver it to them.

You can't harvest a crop unless the ground has been plowed and cultivated, the seeds planted and nurtured until they grow and blossom and bear fruit. After all of that, then you can harvest. It isn't difficult; the fruit often falls into your hand.

Anybody can be a good closer after a good salesperson has done all the necessary preparation.

Since you are doing all the preparation, you might as well harvest the crop; you might as well be the one to have the fun of closing. In a moment we will show you how to use psychorientology to take the fear and stress out of closing.

KNOW WHEN TO CLOSE

If there were a way to know when to close, when the customer is ready to make the decision, you'd probably like to know more about that, wouldn't you?

There is a term for talking too long and passing up the window of opportunity that opens for a short time during a sale. It is called "buying it back." That means that you talked too long and you have bored them.

Emotions build to a peak and at that time the customer is most likely to buy. Sometimes that comes very early, because they already wanted to buy and needed to hear very little from you before deciding to buy from you. Other times, it could take a very long time before they are finally ready to buy.

Like most important things you need to know about during a sales interview, all you need to do to get the answer is . . . ask them: "Are you ready to buy?"

Okay, you usually won't use those words, although they

might very well do the job. Usually you ask them a question that is called a "trial close."

A trial close asks a question about some minor detail. When they answer, you simply watch for the password, or key word that tells you when they have decided to buy your product or service.

"How many of these would it take to meet your needs?" That is a trial close.

If they answer, "I don't know if it will meet my needs," then they are not ready to buy. You need to back up and do some more work. By asking questions, you can find out where the problem is. Have you uncovered their need? Do they have enough desire for the benefits? Do they believe that your product can give them the benefits they desire? Ask questions, and listen to the answers to find out what the problem is.

On the other hand, if they answer, "I will need five, and one more as a backup in case anything happens to one of those five," then they have indicated a readiness to buy. Now work out the details: payment method, delivery date, and so forth.

"That's what you are looking for, isn't it?" is an excellent trial close. "That's what you want, isn't it?"

A trial close reinforces the buying decision. "You like the feel of that, don't you?" "That makes sense, doesn't it?"

Spend some time at your level figuring out various trial closes that you can use for your product or service. Then use them.

GET READY TO CLOSE

When you get satisfactory responses to your trial closes, then you are ready to close.

At this point you can ask a direct question that will move you right into the close, or else will uncover any remaining objections.

"Based on everything we've been discussing, I recommend that you (give your recommendation). What do *you* think?" Then be quiet. Wait for the prospect to speak. If you speak first, you spoil it.

Your prospect will always do one of two things:

1. Tell you that he or she wants to buy, or,
2. Object.

If the prospect wants to buy, take out the order form and write it up.

If the prospect comes out with an objection, then deal with it.

If you do not want to use such a powerful statement, here is a closing question that is used by many Silva Method lecturers, which you can adapt and use for your product or service:

"If time and money were no problem, would you like the benefits that this program offers?"

If you have done your job right, of uncovering their needs and showing them how your product or service will satisfy those needs, then they will almost always answer Yes. Then you move right into the close.

UNCOVERING HIDDEN OBJECTIONS

It is worth mentioning here that people do not always tell you their real objections. This is often part of the flight or fight response; when they buy your product, they are moving into new territory. Remember that we have been programmed biologically to be alert and cautious anytime we encounter anything new. Your prospect fears he or she might be making a mistake. If their objection is never overcome, then they are justified in not buying—not taking a risk.

You are paid to take risks. It is your job to have the courage and confidence to guide them safely to the decision that will improve their life in some way.

How do you know when they are concealing their true objections? Sometimes you can guess this, because there is no logical reason why they should hesitate. Also, you can become so sensitive to people that you can sense that they have some hidden objection. In order to develop this sensitivity, enter your level for fifteen minutes every day, and also practice the techniques that will develop your clairvoyant ability, as discussed in Chapter 14.

With practice, you will not only sense that they have a hidden objection, but you will be able to figure out what the objection is so that you can then ask questions that will lead your prospect through their concerns easily and comfortably.

Then you are ready to close.

THE BEST CLOSE

Most sales books divide closing into categories. This may make the books bigger, but in reality, there is really only one important category:

Assumptive.

You simply assume, and act as if, the person is buying.

Say everything that you say, and do everything that you do, with the idea in mind that the person has already decided to buy. Pretend that the person just told you, "I'll take it, what do we have to do?"

What would you say? What would your attitude be? What would be the very next thing you would do? Would you ask where the merchandise should be delivered? Would you ask if they wanted one of these or two?

Use that attitude when it is time to close and you will give your customers the confidence to make the decision.

To make it easier to use the assumptive close, program it on your Mental Screen first. Go through your sales presentation, right up to the close. Then imagine yourself assuming that the person will agree to your proposal; imagine what they will say to indicate their agreement, and what kind of action they will take to consummate it.

Then on your next sales call, simply recall the image that you created and projected onto your Mental Screen, and expect it to take place. Once you make up your mind, you can't fail; you will succeed. This is how you can use your mind to cause the effects that you desire in your life. Do it at alpha, and you will succeed, as long as it is in everyone's best interest.

HOW THE SUPERSTARS CLOSE

Here is a secret that can help make you a better closer.

Success magazine reported on a survey that tracked hundreds of outstanding salespeople in half a dozen major industries, to determine how they closed.

All of the salespeople in the study were excellent—they had all met their quotas consistently for at least two years. Some of them were much better than others—they were considered superstars.

What was the difference between the excellent salespeople, and the superstars?

In 46 percent of the calls that resulted in orders, the superstars *never* asked for the order.

By contrast, the other salespeople asked for the order more than 90 percent of the time before they got it.

Even when the superstars asked for the order, it was often no more than a nudge, something like, "Let's do it," according to the magazine.

The article suggested that the superstars were better at gaining an understanding of the customer's problem, and stayed with the customer step-by-step through the selling process, so that when they arrived at the conclusion, there was no need to even ask for the order . . . at least 46 percent of the time.

When you do your job properly, then you can assume that your customer is going to take the logical step . . . and buy. This is what José Silva means when he says that a good salesperson is a consultant, who helps the client find what's best.

MORE CLOSING TECHNIQUES

Here are some other closing techniques that you might want to incorporate along with your assumptive close:

1. Alternate proposal.
   "Which would be better for you, to get the combination unit, or the component system?"

   In other words, are you going to buy, or are you going to buy? Instead of thinking about buying or not buying, they think about how to buy. A good alternate proposal gives two seemingly different choices that result in the same outcome.

   Buy or buy.

   Do you want it this way or this way?

   Whether to buy or to buy, that is the question.
2. Minor point.
   "Do you want your name engraved on this, or will you take it as it is?"

   "Do you want to pay by check or credit card?"

   "How do you want your receipt made out?"

   Minor points are just that. They can best be described as one of the minor details that would need to be taken care of after the prospect has decided to buy.

   By asking the customer a detail that is normally taken care of after the sale, you can "help them along." The purpose of using a minor point is to help the customer to choose the right course of action.

   Minor points are easy, simple, and very natural. It is much easier to make a small decision. Don't make a big deal out of it, and it will serve you well.
3. Instructional.

What would you say to a customer who said, "Okay, I'll take it, what do I do now?"

You might say, "Okay, we just need to get this agreement filled out."

"Just make out your check to . . . "

As we said before about the assumptive close, it is very easy to "act as if" they had just decided to buy.

Also, remember what José Silva cautioned about closing: People do not like being told what they have to do, or that they've got to pay. Be cool about it. Do not say, "You have to fill out this form," or "You have to give a $50 deposit." Instead say, "Let's fill out this form," or "Do you want to use a credit card or a check for the deposit?"

PROGRAM YOURSELF FOR SUCCESS

Remember to use all of the mental techniques you have been learning in this book to help you to become a better closer. When you do this, you will remove all of the fear and stress from closing. Your customers will perceive you as relaxed, self-assured, confident, because you will be. Confidence is contagious, and they will readily buy from you.

Here are some techniques to use:

- Use your Mental Screen to practice closing. Eventually you will have done it so often—at the alpha level—that you will feel as though you are one of the most experienced closers in the business. Remember how the field hockey players got almost as much benefit by practicing mentally as those who practiced physically? And remember how those who did both got more than twice as much benefit? Program yourself, then go out and close. When you do both, your progress will surprise your sales manager, and you, too.
- Use your Three Fingers Technique as necessary to help you become a better closer. Pre-program yourself to

use the Three Fingers Technique to remain relaxed when closing, to remember your trial closes, to project a confident attitude, or whatever you sense mentally, at your level, that you need.

- Use the motivation technique you learned in Chapter 9. At your level, think about all of the reasons that you have for making the sale, think of all the people who will benefit. When you have enough motivation— when your desire is high enough—then nothing will stop you from making the sale.

- Practice the relaxation techniques that you learned in Chapter 5. Take a deep breath and relax while you exhale; recall your ideal place of relaxation to relax mentally.

- Practice mental housecleaning, as you learned in Chapter 2. Use words that create positive mental pictures, mental pictures of the desired end result. Praise yourself, the way Coach Chacon praised his basketball players, and you will perform better than ever before.

You now have at your disposal all of the techniques to make you one of the best closers in the business.

Make up your mind to use them, and get to work.

Record Book

This could be the *most important page* in this chapter. All superstar salespeople know the importance of keeping good records. You are a winner, and you will demonstrate it to yourself by recording your progress on this page.

What is the most valuable technique you learned in Chapter 12? _____

How will this technique help you? _____

Why is this important to you? _____

Date used and results: _____

SUCCESSES

Date	Technique Used	Results
_____	_____	_____
_____	_____	_____
_____	_____	_____
_____	_____	_____
_____	_____	_____
_____	_____	_____
_____	_____	_____
_____	_____	_____
_____	_____	_____

13

HOW CUSTOMER SERVICES INCREASE YOUR INCOME

Year after year, struggling salespeople ask the superstars of the business for the "secret of your success."

Year after year, the superstars tell them the secret.

Year after year, the strugglers say, "Oh, yeah. Now . . . tell me the real *secret!"*

When the superstars tell them about making more calls, the strugglers object, and they say that they need to find higher quality prospects in order to increase their sales.

When the superstars tell them to take care of their customers and make sure they are satisfied, the strugglers complain that they are too busy seeking new qualified prospects.

"So please, tell me the real *secret of your success!" the strugglers plead.*

The superstars give up, and tell the strugglers, "I learned to love money, to accept it gratefully. Now I just enter my level, project the amount I want to earn this month onto my Mental Screen, and it happens."

For some reason, the strugglers believe this fiction. They go out and do it, and their sales and income . . . stay the same as before.

"They wouldn't tell me the real *secret," they complain to the other struggling salespeople. "They refuse to share it."*

Mental programming, as you have learned in this book, will increase your effectiveness many times over. But . . . you first have to be doing the things that successful salespeople do.

DO THIS AND YOU'LL NEVER HAVE TO TALK TO STRANGERS AGAIN

Wouldn't it be wonderful if you never had to make another cold call again?

Wouldn't you love to find a way to sell your product or service to 50 percent of the people you approach, instead of just 10 percent?

There is a way. But very few salespeople use it.

Why?

Because they are more interested in making money than in helping people.

Throughout this book, we have said that cooperation produces better results than confrontation.

In the long run, your compensation is directly proportional to the benefits that other people receive from your efforts.

The more people you help, the more money you earn.

What is the big secret that will allow you to completely eliminate prospecting, and to sell 50 percent of all the people you approach instead of just 10 percent?

Take care of your customers.

HOW TO MAKE MONEY BY SERVING YOUR CUSTOMERS

If you don't keep your customers satisfied, somebody else will.

Once you sell your product or service, you'd better stay in touch with that customer to make sure he is satisfied, because if he has any questions or doesn't understand something, if you are not available to answer those questions or resolve anything that goes wrong, he will find somebody else who can. And he won't buy from you again.

Most salespeople are so concerned with the instant gratification of an immediate commission that they forfeit the future wealth that they could have if they would only increase the value of what they do for their customers.

YOU HAVE TO PRIME THE PUMP

A man walking through the desert was desperate for a drink of water. He was certain that he was dying of thirst. Suddenly in the distance he saw an old pump standing by a lone cactus.

He got closer and saw that there was a flask of water there too. On the flask of water was a sign that read, "Danger! Warning!" When he reached the pump, he found that there was a piece of paper attached to the Warning sign. He unfolded the paper and read the following on it:

"Thirsty traveler, you must have faith. There is enough water in this little flask to quench your thirst for the moment, but the next oasis is more than 100 miles distant. You will never make it on this one drink of water; you will surely die if you try. But if you pour this water down the pump, the water will prime the pump, wet the leather washer, and the pump will then provide all the cool, clear water you need."

Salespeople who keep running out looking for immediate gratification, rather than doing what they should be doing, will die of thirst.

That's why salespeople are hard at work in the big cities, seeing and selling lots of new customers, and still dying of thirst.

Some salespeople are like nomads, they wander from wilderness to wilderness opening up new territories. They have to pitch a tent every night.

They are like the Don Juan who promises, "I'll love you forever . . . today." But what happens when tomorrow comes?

Very few salespeople service their clients. After the sale is made, they say, "Thank you for your money because I just made a commission. Call me if you want to buy anything again." They take the money and run, and the customer never hears from them again, except when the salesperson needs to make another sale.

"Hello, Joe, remember me, Charlie Salesman? I sold you that wonderful widget. I was just wondering if you'd like to buy another one?"

These salespeople are like the man who was hiking in the wilderness, when a freak snowstorm blew in. The trail was covered, he was wandering aimlessly, and it was obvious to him that his life was in danger.

When he rounded the bend he saw before him the most beautiful lean-to he had ever seen. It was only a slanted roof coming out of the ground, but it was a much needed shelter.

As he got closer, he became even more excited, because in the corner was the most beautiful old potbellied stove he'd ever seen.

There was actually a box there with kindling wood, some kerosene, and matches.

When the man took his gloves off, he realized how numb his hands were. He held his hands up to the cold stove, and told the stove, "If you will warm me up first, my fingers will feel better and I will be able to strike the matches and warm you up." What do you think happened? His fingers just got colder.

A customer is like that woodstove. You have to warm them up first, then they will be warm toward you. Too many salespeople try to do it the other way. They want customers to keep buying from them, and giving them referrals, without the salesperson having to do anything to earn it.

YOU HAVEN'T COMPLETED THE SALE UNTIL YOU'VE SATISFIED THE CUSTOMER

Selling is service.

"I haven't made a cold call in years," Dave Bellizzi says. That's because he takes care of his customers; he makes sure they are completely satisfied. He wouldn't do business any other way.

"When I started selling," Bellizzi admitted, "all I wanted to do was make money, money, money! And do you know what? With that attitude I only made $5,300 my first year.

"Then I took the Silva Method Basic Lecture Series. I learned how to enter the alpha level, and I learned the laws of programming. I learned that cooperation produces better results than confrontation.

"So I shifted my consciousness from making money, to helping people.

"When I started to look for ways to help people, guess what: The money came in faster than I knew what to do with it!"

JOSÉ SILVA'S PROSPERITY SECRET

José Silva not only endorses this attitude, he teaches it.

"When I need something," he explains, "I enter my level and figure out what new service I can provide that will be of value to people.

"Then I figure out how to provide that service. I develop a plan. And I program myself to do what I have decided on, and to do it in a way that will be of most benefit to the people I want to help."

There is one more step in his prosperity programming:

"You deserve to be compensated for your services," he

said. "The law of balance needs to be maintained. So while I am programming to provide more service, I also keep in mind what my own needs are . . . plus a little bit more."

Keep one point in mind here: You are not compensated for the amount of work that you do. Your compensation is based on the value of your services to the people who receive those services.

It is very hard work to dig a ditch, but the ditch has only a certain value. If you show a business owner a way to save $50,000, then that is going to be worth far more than a ditch. And it may take a lot less effort on your part than digging a ditch.

HOW JOSÉ SILVA WON A NEW CADILLAC

In 1988 José Silva won a new Cadillac in a raffle. He instructed Ed Bernd Jr., editor of the *Silva Method Newsletter*, to write an article about it.

Bernd thought about the graduates who call headquarters from all over the world asking for a technique to win a lottery. "This is all I need," he thought to himself, "to run an article that will lead people to believe that they can program and get something for nothing." Of course, he didn't say this to Mr. Silva. Instead he asked a carefully worded question:

"How did you program to win the lottery?"

The answer was all that he had hoped and expected it to be:

"I didn't," José Silva said. "It just sort of happens."

Bernd asked him to explain what he meant.

"I did not program to win it," Silva told him. "I have been purchasing tickets every year for many years from the Laredo chapter of the Alhambra organization because the proceeds are used to provide help for the local mental health and retardation programs.

"I never program to win," he said. "I just continue to program to fulfill my mission on this planet.

"When Arturo Barrera of Alhambra handed me the keys to the car, I considered that to be a sign that I am doing what I should be doing. It lets me know that those around me are also doing what they should be doing."

He explained that, "Life goes through cycles. It is much like the tide: Sometimes you are riding high, but when the tide goes out, you ride much lower.

"During high tides, abundance comes easily. We feel good, we prosper, and the world looks good.

"During low tides, times are leaner, there is less to choose from, and we must work harder.

"It is important that we also work hard during the high tides," he added, "so that we have a little something extra to help us out during the times when the tide goes out.

"Entering your level every day and centering yourself will help you have a smoother life. The cycles will still be there, but you can manage them better when you are centered.

"When you stay in touch with your source, you receive sound guidance, you make good decisions, and you get positive results.

"When you stay centered, you will know instinctively when you can splurge and when you should save.

"These cycles go beyond our ability to completely control them. Many other people are involved. You may be correcting problems and helping the creator, but others around you may not be. If that is the case, you can be swept along as the tide goes out.

"Of course, when the tide is rising, it will lift you up too, perhaps higher than the others.

"When you are centered, when you are doing the work you were sent here to do, and when others are also fulfilling their mission, and the tide is high, that's when unexpected good things can happen to you."

Speaking of winning the raffle, he continued, "I interpret this to mean that we are on the right track with the Silva Method, that we are moving in the direction we are supposed to go.

"This movement is more than just me. It involves all of us."

Bernd asked jokingly if Mr. Silva were going to share the Cadillac with the rest of the staff. "That car is for my wife," Silva answered. "She needs a new car."

That is not the end of the story. Ever since he won the Cadillac, Silva has increased his contribution to Alhambra by purchasing the $100 raffle tickets for all of the employees at Silva International headquarters. A couple of years later, Omar Cruz, a press operator in the company's print shop, won a $10,000 prize with the ticket that José Silva had given him. Everyone agreed that Cruz was an appropriate winner. He has been a hardworking, dedicated employee for many years, and is the best press operator in the company. He prints virtually all of the Silva Method Basic Lecture Series manuals used in the United States.

AN EASY WAY TO GET REFERRALS

As a salesperson, you are in an excellent position to put the Law of Compensation to work for you. The more valuable you become to your customers, the more compensation you will receive. Sometimes it will be a direct result of your efforts—help a customer and they will refer a new customer to you. Other times, your compensation may come indirectly, as in José Silva's case.

Let's talk about what you should do *after* your prospect signs on the dotted line.

As soon as the prospect signs your order form, he or she goes from being a prospect to a customer. He is making a statement that he likes you, he trusts you, and he believes you.

The first thing to do at this time is to ask for referrals.

Here is how to ask:

"John, I'd like your help." (Pause a few seconds. Timing is important.) "I'd like the names of three of your closest friends. Maybe they, too, would also be interested in my services. I will approach them on the same professional basis that I've approached you." Then get ready to write down their names.

While doing this, use your Mental Screen to imagine your customer giving you names of people who are interested in your services, and being glad that he could help both you and them in this manner.

After you get the names, say two things:

"Would you have any objection if I mentioned your name?"

"If you talk to them in the next couple of days, just mention my name to them."

Then when you call them for an appointment, say, "Bill, my name is (give your name). I'm with the (company name). Did John Doe mention my name to you?" It does not matter if Bill says Yes or No, just proceed with your usual approach.

The chance of a referral buying from you is as high as 50–50. The chance of a stranger buying is 1 in 10.

Which odds do you prefer?

BUILDING A STRONG RELATIONSHIP WITH YOUR CUSTOMER

The next thing you do is to send your customer a thank-you note, thanking them for their business and thanking them for the referrals.

There are companies that market thank-you cards for this purpose. Invest in them. They will pay you back tenfold. Nobody sends thank-you notes . . . except the super successful salespeople.

Customers are really inspired by this. They say, Hey, this salesperson is different. I like that.

You can also send them a card on their birthday. How many people send you a birthday card each year?

IT IS ALWAYS THE RIGHT TIME TO GIVE CUSTOMER SERVICE

Silva Method Lecturer Carolyn Deal of Greensboro, North Carolina, starts providing customer service even before she delivers the product.

Her classes are usually filled up several weeks before the actual course begins. Once a person registers for class, she sends them a form asking what benefits they are seeking from the course.

This helps the students focus their own thinking, so that they are looking for specific benefits. As you learned in Chapter 4, setting specific goals can be a big help in bettering your life.

In addition, Carolyn is better able to work with each student when she knows what benefits they are seeking. During class, she makes it a point to speak with each participant individually to help insure that they are getting the specific benefits they desire out of all the dozens of benefits that the Silva Method offers.

In order to give the kind of personal service she feels is important during the Basic Lecture Series, Deal limits the size of her classes to eighty new participants. And in order to insure that she has enough time to follow up on all of the graduates, she schedules only one lecture series every two months.

How many salespeople do you know who will pass up an extra sale today, in order to provide top-notch customer service? How many salespeople do you know who understand that they can earn more money by doing an outstanding job of satisfying their customers, than by being a good closer? Or to put that same question another way, how many superstar salespeople do you know?

Is it any wonder that Carolyn Deal has been one of the top Silva Method producers in the United States for the last several years?

SERVICE FIRST, THEN SALES FOLLOW

Sister Charlotte Bruck, who lives in St. Mary-of-the-Woods, Indiana, goes one step further: She begins her customer service work before she even creates her product or meets the customer. She does this at her level, as you will learn about in Chapter 14.

The artistic sister says that her greatest urges are:

1. To make someone happy.
2. To help solve someone's problem.
3. To keep thanking God for her many blessings.
4. To share her talents with other people.

Artists are notorious for not being able to sell their work for enough to earn a living. Sister Charlotte is an exception. "I sold sixty-five paintings in about five years, and 4,300 note cards just last year," she said. She does the calligraphy on each card—one at a time. Then she sells them or gives them as gifts. That's quite a lot for a seventy-three-year-old woman who almost died from severe head injuries received in an automobile accident ten years ago.

"I think my qualities for accomplishing the above are determination, risk-taking, positive thinking, faith in God's love for helping me, quick decision-making, continuing my knowledge on a subject to be of better help, and frequent programming at my level for future events."

She doesn't just paint what *she* likes. She enters her level before creating paintings or cards, to help her determine what her customers want. "I always ask the Holy Spirit to help me make decisions on scenes that would make some-one very joyful at first sight," she explained. "I visualize someone looking very happy at the peaceful landscape, and so it happens.

"When I did child portraits," she continued, "I visualized a young mother who would want this for her little boy or girl. I did many from the rear looking out on water, etc. And so it happened. Who will want what? This led me to choose something that someone would really want to buy. And so it happened. I still get comments from Orlando people, where I used to work, who have one of my paintings in their bedroom, workroom, etc. Even the brain surgeon!''

After using her level to discover what people want, how does she sell it?

"Mostly I use the Mirror of the Mind [similar to the technique you learned in Chapter 8], and often use my Lab and Counselors [a technique presented in the Silva Method Basic Lecture Series]."

Sister Charlotte says that when she holds a show to sell her cards, "I imagine the display of cards, and a swarm of people arriving, just trying to get there first for the cards they want. It comes naturally, because it happens every time.

"At a pre-Easter show, I had Easter cards along with eight other kinds, and before a half hour had passed, I had more requests for Easter cards. All sold out! Fortunately, I knew it would happen; so I made extra cards just ready for the outside message, sat down there and did the calligraphy on them.''

Sometimes her programming produces more work than she can handle. "Before Christmas I was so tired that I had to refuse about six large orders from other cities," she said. "I had to go 'out of business' until after the new year. I was bushed!''

TAKE CARE OF YOUR CUSTOMERS, OR SOMEBODY ELSE WILL

After the sale, call your customer within thirty days to see if everything is all right, and to answer any lingering questions they may have. See if they need any help.

How often do salespeople call you after the sale to make

sure everything is all right? If you've ever had one call you, you will probably remember it easily because it is such a rare thing.

Many salespeople are afraid to call because they don't want to hear any possible customer complaints. But if the customer is unhappy, they are going to complain to somebody. Who would you rather have them complain to: you, or other potential customers?

If you get to them first, you can take care of the complaint. Then instead of telling people what a bad deal they got, they will tell everybody who will listen what a great salesperson you are, because you are actually interested in helping them and not just making money.

Research conducted by several major catalog companies shows that customers who complain and then their complaint is taken care of to their satisfaction, often become better customers than those who never complain.

LONG-TERM BUSINESS RELATIONSHIPS BUILD YOUR FORTUNE

Your customers can be a gold mine for you for many years. Remember to prime the pump and you will have an endless supply of water to quench your thirst, and plenty to share with others. Light their fire by calling them and helping them, and they will reward you handsomely as they tell glowing tales about what a good friend you are, as well as a good salesperson.

Set up a routine to call on all of your customers regularly. You should call each one personally at least once a year. Review their needs. See if there are any changes.

People buy new cars regularly, new stereo systems for their homes, new clothes. Families grow and need new insurance, new investment strategies, new homes.

You can even send out annual checkup reminders to clients, the way dentists do, to suggest possible purchases.

Remember that every time you call a customer, you have

the opportunity to get more business, and to get new referrals from them.

Here are a couple of points to remember about phone calls:

Always return someone's call as soon as possible.

If you say you are going to call someone at a certain time, make sure you do it.

When people build up their expectancy, you don't want to let them down. You know what it's like when somebody has hinted at a nice gift they plan to give you for your birthday, and then you don't get it. Be reliable. Your customers like you, they trust you, they believe you. Give them reasons to continue to do so.

Also, remember to respect their needs by asking if they have a moment to talk. Usually they do. If they indicate that they are busy, then ask when it would be convenient to call them back. They will appreciate your courtesy and concern so much that they repay it by paying special attention to what you have to say when you call back.

HOW ONE CALL BENEFITED HUNDREDS OF PEOPLE

Ron Shane has been a test conductor at Cape Canaveral since the 1960s, and has been responsible for launching many missiles. In the early 1970s there were a lot of layoffs at the Cape, and Shane thought he might wind up among them, so he began looking for a business opportunity. Eventually he purchased a franchise for a quick printing business and opened it in Melbourne, Florida.

After a two-week training session, Ron put his wife Georgia in charge of the printshop. Twenty years later, Ron is still launching missiles, and Georgia is still running a very successful business.

Georgia had never even held a job outside the home before. Her job had been raising four wonderful children, and taking care of Ron.

Suddenly, she was the boss of a small printshop.

"When I started, I didn't know anything at all about how to run a business," she said. "But I knew how to be a customer. I knew the way I'd want to be treated, and I always treated my customers that way."

This often meant staying up late at night, and working through the weekend, to get jobs out. When customers complained, she often reprinted the job for free, even if it was not her mistake. Gradually she learned enough about the printing business to be able to manage a very profitable business while working more normal hours.

By the late 1970s, other people were beginning to open quick printing shops. Often these were opened by experienced printers who thought they could do a better job than the housewife. They would attract some of Georgia's customers away with lower prices, but eventually most of those customers came back. "We like the way you treat us," they would say.

Often when Georgia would come across a good idea, something that seemed logical for one of her customers, she would call that customer and tell them about it. The ideas did not always involve printing, but they always made friends.

One idea resulted in the city of Melbourne auctioning off its municipal band.

Georgia heard on the radio about a city that auctioned off a performance of its municipal band as a way to raise money for the band. The next day she called the lady who purchased printing for the Melbourne Municipal Band and told her about the idea.

Several weeks later, the lady came by the printshop. "We've approved your idea," she told Georgia. "We are auctioning off the band."

Georgia protested that it was not her idea, but that made no difference. The band needed raffle tickets, flyers, and other printed materials.

The best part was the auction itself. The winner was a resident of a local nursing home. The concert that the band played on the front lawn of the nursing home on a beautiful autumn Sunday brought out a nice crowd to the nursing home, and brought joy to a lot of elderly people who loved both the music and the company. It was a gratifying experience for everyone associated with the band, and also brought them a lot of publicity.

Is it any wonder that Ron and Georgia Shane have prospered so well in that printshop? One of their daughters now runs the printshop, while Ron and Georgia have more time to themselves.

CUSTOMER SERVICE MOTIVATES YOU

There is another benefit to providing good customer service: It will motivate you, inspire you, and even make you a better closer.

Imagine the good feeling you will have when you know that your customers are doing much better as a result of knowing you. Imagine how that will automatically motivate you to close harder, to hang in there and close more sales.

One good strategy is to start every day by calling some of your satisfied customers. This will motivate you, as well as them.

If you discover that you are not closing strongly enough, and prospects are just walking away without making a decision, go see some satisfied customers and build up your belief in the benefits of your products and services.

When several customers tell you how much they appreciate your calling, and a grateful customer tells you for the umpteenth time how much they appreciate that great idea you gave them, imagine how motivated you will be to go find new customers.

Are you helping them, or are they helping you?

You sell them something and earn a commission. Now help them get the greatest benefit from it, and you will have won a friend; a friend who will become a walking billboard for you, who will become *your* best advertisement, *your* best salesperson, maybe even your best friend. What a way to build your own personal sales force.

That is why superstar salespeople like Dave Bellizzi, Georgia Shane, and others never need to make cold calls.

Would you rather make cold calls, or call satisfied customers?

At your level, build up your desire to serve your customers by thinking of all the benefits of doing this: benefits to your customers, to the friends they will refer to you, to you, your family. Reinforce this often at level; motivate yourself from within to satisfy your customers and keep them satisfied, and you will join the superstar salespeople in the winner's circle. That is what you want, isn't it?

A FORMULA TO MAKE PROSPECTING MORE PLEASANT

Here is a formula to get you started:
Allocate your daily calls in this manner:

1. Make one third of your calls to satisfied customers. Answer their questions; make sure they are satisfied; and obtain referrals from them. This will motivate you and get your flywheel turning. It will give you the momentum to go to the next step.
2. Make another one third of your calls to referrals. Call people whose names you have gotten from satisfied customers. You don't have to sell yourself to them the way you did to the original customer. Your satisfied customer will convince them that they can trust you and will benefit from doing business with you.
3. After you have run out of referrals to call, then make the remainder of your calls to strangers.

It is a lot easier to make cold calls after you have been inspired and motivated by your satisfied customers, and by their friends who are pleased to find somebody like you to do business with. You will not have the attitude that you are taking up their busy time; you will *know* that you are able to help them more than any other salesperson in your field.

Record Book

This could be the *most important page* in this chapter. All superstar salespeople know the importance of keeping good records. You are a winner, and you will demonstrate it to yourself by recording your progress on this page.

What is the most valuable technique you learned in Chapter 13? _____

How will this technique help you? _____

Why is this important to you? _____

Date used and results: _____

SUCCESSES

Date	Technique Used	Results
_____	_____	_____
_____	_____	_____
_____	_____	_____
_____	_____	_____
_____	_____	_____
_____	_____	_____
_____	_____	_____
_____	_____	_____
_____	_____	_____
_____	_____	_____

14

OVERCOMING OBJECTIONS AHEAD OF TIME

Ana Maria Mendez went to her level while Steve Martinez drove. "Stop here," she said suddenly, and Steve pulled to the curb. "This house," she pointed. They went in and sold a set of encyclopedias. Then they got back into the car and went through the routine again.

On one Saturday in May they sold thirty-seven World Book Encyclopedias in a small town in South Texas. "In the next seven weeks," Ana Maria said, "we sold seventy-seven sets of encyclopedias. We helped seventy-seven families."

"We would just drive down a street and she would tell me which house to stop at," Steve said. "When we used the techniques we learned in the Silva Method Sales class, along with her intuition, we couldn't miss!"

HE HAD ALL THE RIGHT ANSWERS

Garry Kann woke up, sat up in bed, and entered his laboratory level. That is a special technique in which a person creates an imaginary workshop for doing mental work. He visualized the group of New York executives he would face in a meeting the next day and thought about the proposal he would make to them.

He questioned them mentally about their goals, their concerns, their way of doing business. He imagined telling them about his product, and imagined what their questions and objections would be. He imagined what they would like about his product, and why.

Then he formulated a specific proposal for these executives, lay down, and went back to sleep.

In the meeting the next day, Garry gave a perfect proposal. He spoke their language, phrased things their way rather than his. He showed them the product both from his point of view and from their point of view.

By the end of the meeting, they liked Garry, they trusted him, believed in him, and they felt that he was better qualified to handle the deal than the other people who had submitted proposals because Garry addressed their specific concerns. They felt that Garry knew more about their business than any of the others.

He made the sale.

FINDING THE BEST SOLUTION

Linda Almaraz entered her level and visualized the couple who wanted to purchase a house in an Oklahoma City suburb. She tried to imagine all the objections they might have.

She realized that the husband wanted to spend only a certain amount of money, but he did not want to let his wife know that this was all he was willing to spend. He had been throwing up false objections to the other real estate agents who had shown houses to them.

"I mentally found out what her needs were, and what his capabilities were, in the form of questions that came to me while case-working the situation," she said, "and then very tactfully brought it up. He was relieved, she was thrilled: we saved his ego, and they got what they wanted to buy."

IMAGINARY WARNING SIGN PREVENTS BIG LOSS

Betty Perry had a buyer for her house in St. Petersburg, Florida. He had made a good offer, and was to sign a contract the next morning. Just to be safe, Betty went to her level and programmed for guidance.

"The next morning in the shower," she said, "I mentally pictured a flashing neon sign with bright letters: 'No deal, no deal.' Fortunately the real estate agent I was working with is a Silva Method graduate. When I told him, he didn't question my decision not to go ahead with the contract."

Five years later, the wisdom of that decision was confirmed when Betty saw a flier from the Florida Real Estate Exchange warning that the FBI was investigating the man she had almost signed the contract with, for defrauding people in Memphis and Tampa.

THE PERFECT COMPETITIVE BID

Rafael Flores went to his laboratory level and asked his counselors how much he should bid to purchase a repossessed house. The imaginary counselors, which he had created with his imagination during the Silva Method Basic Lecture Series, had proven to be a valuable decision-making tool, and he trusted the impressions he got with this technique.

He bid $61,280. The high bid was about $500 more. Flores was not concerned. Even when the high bidder paid the money for the binder, Flores was not concerned.

A week later, the high bidder defaulted, and Flores got the house. He had programmed to bid the right amount, not the highest amount.

THE SECRET OF THE WORLD'S WEALTHIEST PEOPLE

The richest, most powerful people in the world all share two characteristics that 90 percent of the inhabitants of the planet don't have: They do their thinking at the alpha level, and at that level they are able to mentally sense what people are thinking and feeling.

Researcher and writer Napoleon Hill made that observation in 1925 when he wrote that some people's minds rise above the average stopping point and lead them to fame and fortune. He couldn't teach you how to do it, but said that if you can learn to do it, then you can go as far as you want to go. He talked about the brain being like a radio sending and receiving station. Later he admitted that he had a group of imaginary counselors who helped him. He spoke of forming master mind alliances.

Researchers at the Newark College of Engineering in New Jersey discovered and demonstrated in the 1960s that top executives are able to predict the future. The researchers could observe it, but they couldn't teach you how to develop that ability.

That was left for José Silva to do.

Napoleon Hill said that the educator who develops a method to stimulate any mind to go beyond the average stopping point frequently will have conferred the greatest blessing of all time on humanity.

The method is here: The Silva Method.

You have prepared yourself, and are ready to join the 10 percent of people who achieve the great things because they have somehow naturally developed this special mental ability.

You know how to enter the alpha level with conscious awareness. You know how to think at the alpha level, to make better decisions and improve yourself in many ways.

Now you are ready for the next step: to develop your

clairvoyant ability so that you can mentally sense what people need, and sense the best way to fill that need.

You are ready to learn how to actually use your mind to create your own paradise on earth, the way the super successful people do.

Robert L. Shook, author of more than thirty books including *Ten Greatest Salespersons* and *The Perfect Sales Presentation*, has interviewed many of the greatest salespeople in the world. He observed that superstars seem to develop a special sensitivity to people.

In his book *Hardball: High Pressure Sales Tactics That Work* (William Morrow, 1990), Shook insists that super salespeople don't hesitate to use high-pressure selling techniques when it is appropriate to close a procrastinating prospect.

"I've spent hundreds of hours in the field observing the world's number one salespeople in their respective fields who sell insurance, real estate, automobiles, computers, cosmetics, securities—you name it—and when they sense a prospect is procrastinating, they apply high pressure to close the sale," Shook said. "What's really interesting is that nobody resents them for doing it. Now nobody likes to be high-pressured, and if prospects feel high pressure is being applied, they resent it because they feel abused and manipulated. And when people feel that way, they don't buy.

"However, when a professional and experienced salesperson subtly applies high pressure, he or she intuitively reads prospects so well that they aren't offended.

"The top salespeople are able to judge just how far they can go with a particular person, and they know if they go beyond that point, their high pressure won't work—it will backfire and the sale will be lost.

"Now how do they know how far to go with somebody? This is a skill that is developed over a period of time, after years of being on the firing line in front of enough people, enough times. It is not something they are born with any more than a winning quarterback is born with the ability to read opposing defenses or a winning politician is able to read an audience and respond accordingly.

"I sincerely believe that we can all develop the same kind of sensitivity over a period of time. Selling is no different than other fields where people are able to anticipate other people's reactions in advance. It is simply a matter of doing something again and again and having an awareness about what you are doing," Shook said. "The secret, however, is observing what is happening around you and analyze it. By doing this, eventually you will develop an intuition to read your prospects like a book!"

DEVELOPING SENSITIVITY TO PEOPLE

Now, the Silva Method techniques can accelerate the process of developing that sensitivity to people. New Jersey businessman Garry Kann uses a special technique to tune in to his prospects. Here's how:

"On the night of January 27, I started using the broadcasting technique," Garry Kann said. He explained that he would program himself to awaken automatically at the ideal time, sit up in bed, enter his laboratory level, and mentally broadcast to potential clients, that they would be attracted to his start-up investment banking business.

"On January 28, 29, and 30, we literally started getting a flood of phone calls," Kann continued. "Several people who had said they were not interested suddenly called. Two of them wanted to talk to us some more.

"Two other people signed on during the same week. That is, we signed a general proposal letter where we outline what we propose to do, and they give us a check. Well, two checks came in. To us, that's a big deal. With us, one to three transactions a month is a lot, especially since we are in a start-up situation.

"The calls are still coming in," Kann said on February 15. "After about the 4th of February, I stopped broadcasting.

"Up until the time that I started to broadcast, it was

relatively slow. The broadcasting really turned it around.''

What has the use of intuition meant to the new business?

''Since we are in a start-up situation, it is still too early to tell how much money it is worth to us,'' Garry said. ''Just one of these deals could be worth millions of dollars to us over the next few years.

''I can tell you this,'' he added. ''It has meant survival for us. Without the Silva Method techniques, especially using intuition the way we have, we would be out of business by now.''

RESEARCH INTO INTUITION

Intuition is difficult to research, because attitude plays such an important part. Conventional scientists want to conduct experiments without taking into account the attitude of the people involved. They still use a model appropriate to Newtonian physics rather than Einstein's discovery of relativity.

However, there is some research being done that demonstrates E.S.P. in controlled settings.

Some of the most interesting research comes from Cleve Backster, a polygraph expert, who demonstrates in his laboratory in San Diego, California, that even plants respond to the thoughts of human beings.

Backster first discovered this phenomenon when he connected his lie detector to a Dragon Plant. He wanted to learn if a plant would react to stress. When he decided to try to create stress in the plant by burning the leaves, there was a strong reaction on the polygraph machine. The reaction came when Backster *thought* about burning the plant. He never touched it!

Now, Backster can demonstrate that cells from your own body react to your thoughts, even when the cells are many miles away from where you are. White blood cells are especially susceptible to emotion, he said.

But the degree of success is relative to the attitude of the person doing the research. Another scientist who sat and imagined a plant burning got no reaction from the plant. "There is a difference between pretend, and intend," Backster said. "The scientist did not intend to burn that plant." You can read about Backster's exciting research in the book *The Secret Life of Your Cells* by Dr. Robert B. Stone, published by Whitford Press in 1989.

UNIVERSITY RESEARCH SHOWS THAT INTUITION CAN BE TAUGHT

In a research study presented to the American Educational Research Association's 1988 annual meeting, Dr. George Maycock of Appalachian University in Boone, North Carolina, demonstrated that college students who learned the Silva Method "showed a significant increase" in their intuition.

A group of thirty students who took the Silva Method Basic Lecture Series were asked to complete three test instruments before and after they completed the training, Maycock said.

The three tests were:

1. The HCP Profile Test, which determines left- (logical) versus right-brain (intuitive) dominance.
2. The HCP-PSY Test, which determines beliefs and experiences about intuition.
3. The Intuitive Potentials Test, which measures an individual's current intuitive potentials.

The results of these tests were compared to a control group of thirty individuals who did not take the Silva Method training but were instead enrolled in an education course.

"The individuals who completed the Silva Method training," Maycock reported, "showed a significant increase in scores for all three tests.

"This showed that they tended to become more right-brain or intuitively oriented, their beliefs became more positive toward intuitive thinking, and their potential for intuitive thinking improved.

"Individuals in the control group who did not participate in the training showed no significant gains in scores on any of the tests."

Maycock said that 83 percent of the students showed gains in intuitive abilities.

Of the five students who did not show gains in intuitive abilities, four of them (13 percent of the test group) were already functioning in a high intuitive mode before the training, Maycock said.

"It was also found that those individuals who were left-brained or logic oriented prior to the training tended to benefit the most, since the Silva Method training enabled them to become more intuitively oriented or more balanced in their thinking styles," Maycock noted.

"One researcher," Maycock continued, "found that seventy percent of gifted or high IQ students were predominantly intuitive, while only thirty-nine percent of students in regular classes were intuitive.

"If intuition has been shown to be useful for creativity and success, then both teachers and their students need to be trained to fully use their intuitive abilities.

"The present research study using the Silva Method shows that a training program does exist that can improve right-brain intuitive abilities," Maycock concluded.

INTUITION HELPS IN EVERY AREA OF LIFE

Two Arizona psychotherapists report that the Silva Method techniques help them to get the kind of results you would expect from veteran sales professionals.

They say that the Silva Method techniques have helped them to attract more business, earn more money, be better therapists, get along better with colleagues, invest their money more wisely, serve humanity better, and frequently "do the impossible" in their business.

They program daily, and practice special techniques that make it easy for them to get help from the other side, from the spiritual dimension. They have reached the point that it often happens automatically for them.

"We took the Silva Method course in 1982 to learn intuition and healing, in order to become better therapists," Joan McGillicuddy and Antonio Estrada wrote to José Silva. "We received those benefits and a whole lot more."

First, they attracted more business "because our healing skills improved."

They also attract more business because they know how to get help from the other side.

"Whenever we submit a bid to provide services under a government contract or business contract, we use our Mental Screen to receive that contract, 'or something better,' " they explain.

"One day we submitted a proposal that was to be quite lucrative financially. The proposal was delivered four minutes late, and therefore not accepted. We kept programming, and soon learned that no other proposal was deemed adequate.

"The bidding process was reopened," they said, "and our bid was accepted, allowing us to serve hundreds of people, and with enough income to allow us to purchase an office building for our practice."

Next they programmed the perfect location for the building, as well as the size and price. They had what they wanted in three days: the perfect size building, near the schools where many of their clients come from. And the seller reduced his price by $20,000.

They have programmed very successfully to locate the best investments for the money they are earning.

Serving clients better, and making more money, are only two of the ways that McGillicuddy and Estrada benefit from the Silva Method techniques. They gain many personal benefits as well.

"When we attend business meetings, we program for harmony and the best for everyone involved," they said.

"We have very few conflicts with colleagues.

"We also have noticed that we are definitely sent to where we are needed to correct problems," they continued. "When one contract ends, there is always something better behind it. We do not fear or worry about finances because we know we are being helped to serve humanity. We are open to receive the abundance of the universe.

"We seem to be able to do the 'impossible' in our business. Halfway through the fiscal year, one of our state administrative agencies called to say there was excess funding and we could have our choice of funds from $30 to $150,000! This supposedly 'never happens,' particularly in these days of 'cutbacks.'

"Also, among approximately eight competitors in the area, we are the only ones who can work with this administrative entity."

McGillicuddy says that they go to level every night. "I usually go to level sitting up in bed," she said. "I work health cases and program for the next day."

TEST YOUR INTUITION

The health cases are especially exciting for the therapists, because they use them in their practice.

Before the conclusion of the Silva Method Basic Lecture Series, every participant has an opportunity to work at least ten health cases, more if they want to.

The participant is given the name and age of someone they don't know, who is not present, and they use their mind to sense what kind of health problems that person has.

When they are able to obtain this information, which is not available to their physical senses, then they know that they have learned to use their intuition.

How accurate are participants in the Basic Lecture Series? Approximately 80 percent!

Once they have verified that they were accurate at sensing the information, then they imagine the subject in perfect health. You can learn how effective this is by reading José Silva's book *You the Healer*, published by H. J. Kramer.

All of the people we have talked about in this chapter work health cases regularly to keep their intuition sharp.

"My biggest problem right now," Garry Kann said, "is that I can't get enough health cases. We have established a hot line. Without a doubt, health cases have helped us to accomplish what we have."

Joan McGillicuddy says that she works approximately five new health cases per week, "plus those I work while doing therapy."

DEVELOPING POSITIVE PERSONALITY TRAITS

McGillicuddy and Estrada both practice the Long Relaxation Exercise every day. They frequently use cassette tapes for self-programming.

Both McGillicuddy and Estrada program themselves to develop personal characteristics.

"I programmed to overcome the fear of what people think of what I say and do," McGillicuddy said. "I felt that my apprehension and concerns were weakening my effectiveness when dealing with people. So I programmed myself to say the right thing, and to do the right thing.

"Two days later, a lady told me, 'You're very powerful.' This showed me that the programming worked."

"I use the Three Fingers Technique a lot," Estrada said. "I pre-program myself before a counseling session, to say the right things. I do the same when we are going into negotiations."

"Dream Control is another technique that has helped us," McGillicuddy said. "I use it to decide whether to take on a person as an associate."

Remembering names is another area they have worked on at level, using the Silva Method techniques.

"We find that we always get what we program for," they concluded. "Sometimes it takes longer than other times, but we always get it."

INTUITION IS A NATURAL HUMAN ABILITY

Virtually everyone has flashes of intuition. But Wilfred often rationalizes it away.

Have you ever heard the phone ring and somehow you knew who was calling?

Have you ever had a pre-cognitive dream—dreamed of something and then it happened the next day, or a few days later?

Have you ever had a dream that gave you an idea to solve a problem?

Have you ever gone someplace new and felt like you had been there before?

Can you sometimes guess what someone is going to say before they say it? Or do before they do it?

Do you find that sometimes your guessing ability is better than others?

Most people answer Yes to one or more of those questions.

Let's find out direct from José Silva, the world's leading researcher on intuition, how you can develop your own intuitive abilities for better health, success, and happiness.

HOW TO DEVELOP YOUR INTUITION

We have not been able to find a reliable way to teach intuition in a book or on tape. Sometimes it might work, but often it doesn't.

It takes a mind to educate another mind. A book does not have a mind. A tape recorder does not have a mind. A human being has a mind.

But not just any human being's mind can teach another

to use intuition consciously and on demand. The teacher must be one who can use his or her mind intuitively whenever they desire.

However, there are things that you can do to increase your intuition.

The most obvious thing that you can do to increase your intuitive abilities is to be aware of when you have an intuitive experience, and reinforce it at your level.

Let's say that you are thinking about your clients, and who you should call. Then the phone rings and the person you were thinking about is on the phone. Or you place the call and your client says, "I was just thinking about calling you."

As soon as you can after this, enter your level and review exactly what happened, and especially review how you felt when you were thinking about the person, and when they called.

Eventually you will learn to recognize this special feeling, so that you can take advantage of it. You might even learn how to evoke this special feeling and cause it to happen when you need to use your intuition.

Another thing that you can do to increase your intuitive factor is to enter your level before going to see a prospect and try to figure out what they are going to say, what their objections will be, and how you can best overcome them, what they will like about your product or service.

When you go to see them and find that your guesses were accurate, then as soon as possible after your meeting, enter your level and review the experience as I instructed you above.

This trial and error method might take a while, but it does provide you with a method to develop your intuition.

There is a better way:

Attend the Silva Method training. In forty hours you will have opened the door to a whole new world. You will be able to move around mentally in the spiritual dimension, and get help from the other side, the spiritual dimension.

You can get answers there that are not available to you on this side. It reminds me of a story that I like to tell:

A farmer had three sons. When he died he left a will that stipulated that his estate must be divided in the following manner: The eldest son would get one-half, the second one-fourth, and the third son one-sixth. He added that when they divided up his cattle, they must not butcher any of the cows.

There was a problem: He left 11 cows, and you cannot divide 11 cows into one-half, or one-fourth, or one-sixth, without butchering any cows.

Then someone came up with an idea: They would borrow one spiritual cow, from the other side, and add it to the other 11, giving them a total of 12 cows. Then one-half would be 6, one-fourth would be 3 (6 + 3 = 9), and one-sixth would be 2 (9 + 2 = 11). Now they could return the spiritual cow back to where they got it from.

My research reveals that all of the super successful people in the world get help from the other side. That's only 10 percent of the people on the planet. The other 90 percent are limited to what is available in the physical dimension.

Please, for your own sake, as well as for the sake of humanity, learn to use your intuition, learn to get help from higher intelligence on the other side, and join me and millions of Silva Method graduates who are helping to make this planet a better place to live.

YOUR FUTURE IS UP TO YOU

You have read a lot of documented, true success stories in this book, stories about people who have overcome personal problems, eliminated fears and insecurities and become powerful, persuasive individuals, who have learned to sell, increased their sales, started their own businesses, turned failure into success, increased their success beyond their wildest dreams, and achieved the kind of happiness that everyone desires.

What do *you* want?

What kind of future do you want?

You can have it!

You can have anything you want, if it does not harm anyone else, and if you are willing to do the necessary work.

We guarantee it. The Silva Method has always offered a full, no-questions-asked moneyback guarantee to anyone who is not satisfied at the completion of the Basic Lecture Series. If we weren't satisfying people, we wouldn't still be here.

YOU CAN HAVE ANYTHING YOU WANT

Let us leave you with one final story.

This is a story about a teenager who attended the Silva Method Basic Lecture Series in Corpus Christi, Texas, a couple of years ago.

The program began on Saturday morning, and the lecturer was letting participants introduce themselves and, if they wanted to, tell why they were there.

When the teenager's turn came, he stood up, gave his name, and grumbled, "I am only here because my father made me come. And when I found out how much he spent to send me here, I cussed him out, because he could have used that money to help buy me a car!" Then he flopped back into his chair, slumped down, folded his arms, and stared at the wall.

Throughout the day Saturday, and all day Sunday, the teenager sulked. He kept to himself during breaks, did not ask any questions during class, and clearly conveyed the message that he really didn't want to be there.

When the group returned the following Saturday for the second half of the program, there was no change in the teenager. While everyone else was standing up and sharing exciting success stories about using the Silva Method techniques to program for various things, the teenager continued to sulk, arms folded, looking like an angry young man.

This continued all day Saturday. But the third day of the

Basic Lecture Series is unique; it is something special, because you actually experience functioning with full awareness and conscious control in another dimension. The day concludes with the creation of a mental workshop—we call it a laboratory—and two helpers—we call them counselors.

When it was time to start the final day of class on Sunday morning, the teenager stood up and asked to address the group again.

"Last week," he began, "I said that I didn't want to be here, and I had cussed my father out because that money could have helped me buy a car.

"I want to apologize," he continued. "I apologized to my father last night, because now I realize that when he sent me here, he *did* buy me a car . . . and a stereo . . . and a college education . . . and a career . . . and a family . . . and . . . and . . . anything I'll ever want for the rest of my life!"

Now you have the tools, both physical and mental, to help you get whatever *you* want for the rest of your life.

Now it is up to you to use them.

Make up your mind to practice what you have learned.

Make up your mind to develop your intuition.

Make up your mind to practice going to your level every day.

Make up your mind to be a winner.

And please, share your successes with us.

Record Book

This could be the *most important page* in this book. All superstar salespeople know the importance of keeping good records. You are a winner, and you will demonstrate it to yourself by recording your progress on this page.

Of all the techniques presented in this book, which one are you going to practice next? _____

How will this technique help you? _____

Why is this important to you? _____

Date used and results: _____

SUCCESSES

Date	Technique Used	Results
_____	_____	_____
_____	_____	_____
_____	_____	_____
_____	_____	_____
_____	_____	_____
_____	_____	_____
_____	_____	_____
_____	_____	_____
_____	_____	_____

If you would like to receive the *Sales Psychorientology Newsletter* and information about upcoming Silva Method seminars, contact the Silva Method Sales Training Program at 1-800-545-MIND (1-800-545-6463), or write to 1407 Calle del Norte, P.O. Box 2249, Laredo, TX 78044-2249, or fill out and mail the attached order form.

For a free brochure and information about Silva Method seminars in your area, contact:

Silva International, Inc.
1407 Calle del Norte
P.O. Box 2249
Laredo, TX 78044-2249

Phone: 1-800-545-6463
　　or　　210-722-6391
Fax:　　210-722-7532

Please send me information about Silva Method seminars in my area.

Name _____

Address _____

City/State/Zip _____

Phone (_____)_____

Best time to call: _____